Whose Water Is It?

Whose Water Is It?

THE UNQUENCHABLE THIRST
OF A WATER-HUNGRY WORLD

Edited by **BERNADETTE McDONALD** and **DOUGLAS JEHL**

NATIONAL GEOGRAPHIC
WASHINGTON, D.C.

Library of Congress Cataloging-in-Publication Data

Whose water is it? : the unquenchable thirst of a water-hungry world / edited by Bernadette
McDonald and Douglas Jehl.
    p. cm.
ISBN 0-7922-6238-7
  1. Water-supply. 2. Water conservation. I. McDonald, Bernadette, 1962- II. Jehl,
Douglas.

TD345.W58 2003
333.91--dc21

2003056234

Interior design by Melissa Farris
Printed in U.S.A.

CONTENTS

PREFACE

Paul Simon

For nearly ten years I have been an advocate on the critical issue of our water resources, and I have seen little movement forward in the public consciousness of this ever more urgent situation. I fear for the future of water—and humanity— if people continue on the course that has been set: using water at a rate faster than it can be replenished, wasting water, making multiple claims on the same reservoir, failing to consider the consequences of overuse on the environment and future supply of this invaluable resource, and failing to move ahead on finding less expensive ways of converting salt water to fresh water and on construction of desalination plants. Failure to act courts disaster.

The United States is fortunate. It has 4 percent of the world's population and 8 percent of its fresh water. Canada is in even better shape, with less than one percent of the world's population and 9 percent of its fresh water. But even in these two nations there are distribution problems, with areas like the southwestern part of the United States facing serious water shortages despite the nation's relatively abundant supply.

And the world situation will have an impact on North America in hundreds of ways. Periodically the American intelligence community makes an assessment for the President of the United States of where the country will be in 15 years. Shortly before he left office, President Bill Clinton was given this report and it said that in 15 years—now less than that—the world's great resource shortage will not be in oil but in water, and it predicted regional wars over water, wars that will inevitably involve the United States, at least economically.

Water disputes between nations will only increase in number as water becomes more scarce. The United States has over a hundred ongoing water disputes with Canada. We will not go to war with each other, but that is not necessarily true of many other nations that face serious problems with their neighbors.

There are more than six billion people on the Earth today and, depending on whose forecast you take, 50 to 100 years from now there will be a leveling off of the world population at approximately 11 billion people. On a graph, the population line would be moving up dramatically. Another line on that same graph that would show the Earth's freshwater supply would be flat. This means calamity unless we alter both our habits and our plans for the future. Changing these habits and plans will require people to conserve water, to reuse it, and to tap into the 97 percent of the world's water supply that is salt water. Of the remaining three percent, our fresh water, two-thirds is tied up in icebergs and snow; currently we are living on one percent of the Earth's water.

One of the world's concentrations of water stress (the combination of high population and low supply) is in the Middle East. In the summer of 2003, I returned from a trip to Israel where I moderated a two-person panel composed of Israeli Water Commissioner Shimon Tal and Palestinian Water Commissioner Nabil El-Sharif. Both understand the severity of the deteriorating water situation in that area. Israel primarily relies on three aquifers—two large ones and one smaller one—for its water supply, aquifers that overlap the boundaries of their neighbors because underground water supplies do not mirror artificial political boundaries. These aquifers are declining in quantity, and as they decline saline and other elements penetrate them, impairing the quality of the water. Israel has the highest water quality standards in that region, but they are now not as high as in the United States and Western Europe, and unless large desalination plants are constructed soon the situation will continue to deteriorate both for Israel and her Arab neighbors. The two water commissioners found themselves in substantial agreement—something that does not happen enough in that region. Former Israeli Prime Minister Shimon Peres concluded that water would either be a catalyst for peace or a catalyst for war.

Two years before my visit to Israel, at the request of the State Department, I went to Jordan and Syria to meet with their leaders on water problems, hoping to obtain their cooperation on a regional approach to water where they would work with the Israelis and the Palestinians. Though the leaders acknowledge that the situation will require cooperation among the nations of that region, the countries silently continue to slip toward disaster. When I was in Amman, Jordan, a city of one million, residents were permitted to turn the tap on one day a week. Will the harsh realities of their situation permit them to overcome the barriers to regional cooperation?

And it is not only a quantity issue that the world faces, but also one of quality. One of the editors of this book, Bernadette McDonald, cites that 10,000 to 20,000 children *a day* die because of water that is infected with disease. An international agency uses a slightly more conservative figure, 9,500. Even if you apply that lower number, it means that each day 630 times as many children in the world die because of poor quality water than were killed at the tragedy at Columbine High School in Colorado on April 20, 1999. We were stunned by the Columbine episode, as we should have been, but each day the less dramatic deaths of hundreds of times more children do not disturb us.

This collection attempts to awaken us to a crisis that is creeping upon us and soon will be leaping upon us. I hope that efforts like these continue. If we are informed, we may act.

August 2003

INTRODUCTION

Douglas Jehl

I n April 2003, the American troops from the 101st Airborne Division who entered the town of Najaf after the fall of Saddam Hussein's regime heard immediately what the townspeople wanted most. Was it food, freedom, or retribution, after so many years of repression? No, wrote Jim Dwyer of the *New York Times,* who was accompanying the troops. What the Iraqis in the Euphrates River town wanted was water, that substance most essential to life itself.

The urgent cry in Najaf was the product of a temporary

shortage. But it is an emblem of a broader, unquenchable human thirst, and one that has begun to collide for the first time with real and worrying limits. Until recently, water shortages were relatively rare and isolated. But now, across a widening swath of the world, the strains are becoming both frequent and intense. For decades the world's demand for water has soared even faster than population growth, against finite water supplies. Current trends cannot be sustained much longer; something has to give.

Whose water is it? For most of history, that question must have seemed as abstract and arcane as those involving angels and the heads of pins. But the question is one that suddenly seems to matter very much. Consider another case from the Euphrates, this one from a Syrian village near the Turkish border, hundreds of miles upriver from Najaf. Here, the Syrian government has promised to triple in size the farmland served by irrigation, bringing the river's bounty to farmers forced to eke out a hardscrabble living from the arid earth. But Turkey, Syria's neighbor to the north, has begun an even grander irrigation project that draws from the Euphrates, and the river's flow is not sufficient to satisfy all the dreams. Under the hot summer sun, a Syrian farmer who still hopes for the day the Euphrates will reach his fields tells a visitor that he used to pray to God for help, but now he fears that is not enough. "It's not God who has our water," he says. "It's the Turks."

If water is becoming increasingly scarce, is that bound to ignite clashes between neighbors, farms and cities, or even between countries? That is certainly a real and growing possibility. Kofi Annan, the UN Secretary-General, summed up that sentiment in

2001 when he said that rivalries over water "may well become a source of conflict and wars in the future." But there is another possibility, too. As Mr. Annan hastened to add in separate remarks the next year, there is also the possibility that the world's water problems might become "a catalyst for cooperation," one that could begin to bridge even great divides.

What exactly is the world's water crisis all about? At the most basic level, more and more people are vying for less and less water, in disputes that are growing more rancorous by the day. From China to India to the United States, water supplies are under strain as never before, running dry because of accelerating demands from fast-growing cities, agriculture, and industry. Aquifer levels are falling precipitously, being siphoned toward extinction by electric and diesel pumps. Major rivers like the Colorado, the Yellow, and the Nile no longer flow reliably to the sea, their waters diverted, in large measure, to irrigate infertile lands and feed hungry populations. At work is a toxic combination of population growth, soaring water use per person, and increased pollution, whose combined effects have begun to claim even more water than even abundant resources can provide.

The assessments that have emerged in recent years from international organizations and Western intelligence agencies are chilling. Around the globe, more than a billion people—nearly 20 percent of the world's population—lack adequate supplies of fresh water, according to the United Nations. The dwindling water supply is likely to inhibit economic growth, the World Bank has said, and the effect could be intensified by global warming. By 2015, the U.S. government has estimated, perhaps 40 percent of the world's population, or about three billion people, will live in countries where water is in short supply. By the middle of the century, according to the worst case projected by the United Nations, that number could climb to as many as seven billion people in 60 countries—more people than live in the world today. The United Nations has declared 2003 to be the International Year of Freshwater, but that was hardly a gesture of celebration; "a serious water crisis" is under way, the UN warned, and is "getting worse, and will continue to do so, unless corrective action is taken."

To appreciate the magnitude of the water challenge, let us briefly consider some arithmetic. Seventy percent of the Earth's surface is water, but more than 97 percent of that water is too salty for use in drinking or irrigation. Of the 2.53 percent that is left, more than three-quarters is frozen, locked away as ice in Antarctica and Greenland or in Alpine mountain glaciers. Less than one percent of all the planet's water is both unfrozen and fresh, and (because much of it is inaccessible, usually because it is buried too deep underground), less than half of one percent is available for human consumption, either as groundwater or surface water in rivers, lakes, and streams.

In a sense, of course, fresh water is limitless; it is cycled between the Earth's atmosphere and surface so that it never really runs out. What falls from the sky either evaporates, is frozen as ice or snow, runs off the surface quickly into surface waters, is absorbed by plants, or percolates into the ground, recharging aquifers. This means the natural supply of freshwater is replenished continuously. But it is also finite, in that it cannot be used faster than it is replenished. Unfortunately, overuse is widespread today, not just in arid parts of the Middle East and Asia, but even in areas of the world with abundant rainfall.

Consider, for example, the case of the Ogallala Aquifer, the United States' largest source of underground water, which supplies some of the richest farmland in the country, across eight states from South Dakota to Texas. Since the 1940s, an orgy of pumping fueled by electricity and diesel has siphoned so much water from the aquifer that its levels in many places have dropped by more than 10 feet, and by more than 100 feet in parts of Texas. Although some aquifers recharge relatively quickly, others can take thousands of years to refill, if at all. The Ogallala contains what many call "fossil water"—water that was deposited near the end of the last ice age, 10,000 years ago, and for practical purposes is not being replaced today. At the current unsustainable rate of consumption it is only a matter of time before the Ogallala's wells go dry.

And consider, again, the case of the Euphrates River, which flows more than 1,000 miles from the mountains of central Turkey through Syria and Iraq and into the Persian Gulf. It is a mighty and monumental waterway, whose abundance helped to fertilize ancient Mesopotamia, and for now it does flow all the way to the sea. But in rival blueprints for the future, it is over-subscribed by the three countries that share its banks, whose competing visions of vast irrigation projects that might help to feed soaring populations do not add up to a sustainable river. Their differences have been apparent for nearly a decade, but so far the main outcome has been rancor.

Fresh water serves little purpose, of course, unless it is clean. Pollution, which affects water quality, should also be recognized as having effectively cut into water supplies. In many parts of the world, the cost of providing adequate sanitation and water-treatment facilities is more than governments can bear. The United Nations has vowed that by 2015 to reduce by half the 2.5 billion people who do not have access to basic sanitation services, yet it has so far been able to claim little or no progress.

Still, it is important to understand that the world is nowhere close to running out of fresh water; even the most dire assessments suggest that today's population consumes about half of available freshwater supplies. The basic problem is less one of supply than distribution, because most of the fresh water is located where people are not, in places like the Amazon Basin, and vice versa. Rainfall in the United States, for example, is abundant compared with most other parts of the world, with portions of the country receiving more than 30 inches a year. But although nearly 60 percent of the precipitation falls east of the Mississippi River, the country's booming new centers of population growth are in the West, and some of them, such as Phoenix and Las Vegas, get less than five inches of rainfall a year. It is not only cities, but also agriculture, recreation, and even the environment (through ever more stringent laws) that are staking claims for increased water in the region, setting up for what the Interior Department, in a new report, describes as a stage set for future contention. "Today, the American West is the fastest growing region of the country," the department said in the report, "Water 2025." "Water is its scarcest resource."

Is there any reason for hope? Thankfully, yes. If there is enough water to go around, and the problem is in how it is used, then the crisis is primarily "one of water governance, essentially caused by the ways in which we mismanage water," according to the United Nations. A shift in either the supply or the demand curve could ease the strains and avert a rupture, and there have been signs of progress on both fronts.

No one likes limits, particularly when it comes to water, when every rainstorm, indeed every twist of the tap, brings an illusion of abundance. If there is not enough water now, it is tempting to think, there must be a dam to be built, a glacier to be towed, an ocean to be desalted, a river to be moved—some way to harness technology and ingenuity to fill the void. Certainly, that has been the history of human experience with water, particularly over the past century, as the damming of rivers (think Hoover Dam on the Colorado), the construction of aqueducts (think about the one that feeds Los Angeles, over a course of hundreds of miles), and the mining of aquifers (think, again, about the Ogallala) have defied nature to bring water where it is needed, in the United States and around the world. The idea that the future might bring more such triumphs is hard to shake, and indeed it may be possible one day that seawater can be desalinated cheaply enough to make it a greater part of the world's water equation, or that the waters of a vast river might be successfully rerouted from one part of a country to another, as China hopes to do in transferring water from its water-rich south to its arid northern plains.

But in general, the easiest of such tasks have already been accomplished, and those that remain face daunting obstacles. In the short term, say experts like Peter H. Gleick of the Pacific Institute for Studies in Development, Environment, and Security in California, the costs of trying to add to water supplies will almost always exceed those of reducing demand. Indeed, the effect of environmental laws in the United States in particular is reducing the available supply. Perhaps it is wiser, then, to accept limits and embrace them, as, Mr. Gleick argues, there is the possibility of a soft landing in which the world can find ways to do more with less water without losing out in terms of economic growth.

In trying to do just that, the United States has been a path breaker; per-person water use among Americans has declined by about 10 percent since 1980, more than making up for the effects of population growth. In certain cities, such as Los Angeles and others served by the Southern California Metropolitan Water District, the decline has been particularly notable, with over-all water use declining even as populations soar. If those trends could begin to be replicated more widely, in the United States and around the world, at least some of the pressure would soon ease.

But the obstacles to reducing the demand for water are daunting, to say the least. Improvements in efficiency can be costly in terms of the outlays required for new toilets, improved irrigation systems, or new manufacturing equipment. Raising the price of water, even to something closer to its true value, can dissuade waste, but it brings with it the risk of a political backlash, particularly in developing countries where price hikes would be difficult for many citizens to bear. There is much potential for curbing the water demand, but solutions that have begun to work in the United States may well not make economic sense in India or China, at least not for a long time.

Perhaps the greater barrier to changing the way water is managed, however, lies in attitudes and laws rather than technology. In the farmland around Lubbock, Texas, a region that draws its water from the vast Ogallala, the idea of water conservation has been a mission of the local water district for more than 50 years. And yet, under Texas law, there is no limit to how much water a farmer can pump from the ground beneath his fields, as long as it is put to reasonable use. His only cost is the energy required to pump the water to the surface. Every drop that is pumped, of course, reduces the overall level of the aquifer, but there is no requirement that withdrawals be limited to what can be sustained in the long term. Instead, what takes place is a kind of race to pump the available water before someone else does, and so the level of the aquifer continues to decline, a casualty of self-interest misunderstood.

Whose water is it? The phrase serves as a useful jumping-off place, a way to consider some important corollaries. Might shortages bring scarcities in food supplies as well? Who should take the lead in trying to combat water scarcity? Who will be the winners and losers in water conflicts? Should water be bought and sold, like any other commodity? Is water property, and can a water right be abridged?

Whose water is it? There are no easy answers, and perhaps none are entirely right. But one does seem wrong, if only because it sends exactly the wrong signal, and that is the idea that water belongs to no one, in the sense that no authority should be permitted to restrict its use. Today, perhaps, some water may be mine, some yours, and the rest someone else's. But in the grandest sense, water in the end does belong to everyone, which makes it worthy of hard choices, because without them, quite assuredly, there will one day no longer be enough.

OWNERSHIP

n Cochabamba, Bolivia's third largest city, officials decided in 1999 to put water services under the control of a subsidiary of Bechtel Corporation, a profit-making enterprise. The reasoning seemed eminently sensible: The water system was dilapidated; the government lacked adequate money for new investment; an infusion of private capital would improve services while bringing the discipline of the free market to what had become a costly and inefficient enterprise.

But what happened in practice provoked a popular rebellion.

The private company, Aguas del Tunari, raised the price of the water out of reach of the vast majority of the population, and even gave the company the right to charge for water people took from their own wells. The protests that followed brought hundreds of thousands to the streets, paralyzing the city, and eventually led the Bolivian government to end its contract with the foreign consortium, forcing Bechtel out of the country. Water services in Cochabamba are once again being run on a not-for-profit basis.

Cochabamba has not been the only setting for such protests. Vast numbers of people have also demonstrated in other parts of Bolivia and in Ecuador, Panama, South Africa, and elsewhere, a sign of how highly charged the issue of water ownership has become. At issue is this fundamental question: Should water, a substance close to life itself, be used as a source of profits?

Around the world, private corporations own or operate water systems that earn 200 billion dollars a year. So far they serve only about 7 percent of the population, but despite the backlash in places like Cochabamba, the numbers are increasing quickly. At the heart of the trend is the revolution in thinking that is emerging with the recognition that water is not limitless. But how that should be put into practice is being disputed in villages, cities, and countries all around the globe. Economics tells us that scarcity has value, but does that mean that water, regarded for millennia as essentially free and boundless, should now be bought and sold like any other good?

Who owns water, after all? Is it the property of governments, companies, private individuals, or no one at all? Who, if anyone, has the right to tell a property owner to limit his use of a river, a lake, or an aquifer? What recourse, if any, should a citizen have if a company, a government, or a neighbor takes away the water on which he relied?

More broadly, is water a resource so "essential to life," as Hannah Griffiths of the environmental group Friends of the Earth has put it, that it should be treated as a universal right, with every person guaranteed the "fundamental right" to a clean, healthy supply? Or, because its supply is limited, should it be treated as a commodity and priced to reflect its value so that it will not be wasted? Or does the answer lie somewhere in between, a public good subject to regulation but also to the market, so that its price can serve as a bulwark against waste and can help recoup more of its increasing cost?

These are some of the questions addressed in the essays that follow, which consider water ownership from three perspectives. Robert Glennon writes about a private company that takes advantage of water laws to siphon vast quantities of groundwater in a way that would never be permitted from a river or stream. Marq de Villiers writes about a government whose staggering plan is to transfer a river's flow from one region to another, with enormous consequences for populations at both ends. Maude Barlow focuses on the privatization of water, including the failed attempt in Cochabamba, to question whether water should ever be the province of a profitmaking enterprise.

Among American cities now facing that question is Atlanta, which in early 2003 scrapped (for reasons of poor service) an experiment that put its water-distribution system in private hands. But economic pressures mean that attempt will not be the last; in the United States alone, cities may be facing as much as 500 billion dollars in new costs over the next two decades to serve growing populations, according to the Environmental Protection Agency. For now, American water systems still lag far behind other utilities, like electricity, in the extent of private ownership, but cities including Stockton, California, and Indianapolis, Indiana, have joined the march, contracting out at least some services to private companies.

Will allowing private enterprise to manage or own more of the world's water systems help to overcome the staggering economic problems, which have resulted in part from years when water was sold at enormous discounts? Or will it add to the problems, including those that could subject the poor to impossibly high water bills? On these issues a vast divide remains. The World Bank has been the most outspoken in promoting privatization, while others, including opponents of globalization, are fighting hard to stop it.

When the issue reaches global water policy meetings, as it has repeatedly over the past 20 years, the debate often comes down to one of definitions. Should access to water be endorsed by governments as a human need, as it has been until now, or should it be considered a human right, one that cannot be abridged? The distinction has enormous implications, which is the reason that it has been so hotly debated, most recently at a 2003 conference in Kyoto, Japan, but the polemical dispute threatens to obscure the most important reality.

Whose water is it? Whether it is yours or mine, everyone's or no one's, a first step in thinking about it must be to recognize that it is limited. Markets, for all their flaws, at least offer the virtue of coming to terms with scarcity. People remain too ready to believe that somehow water will always be abundant. If access to water is a human right, it cannot be a boundless one. Buying and selling, within limits, at least drives home the lesson that using water always has a price.

BOTTLING A BIRTHRIGHT?

Robert Glennon

In 1999, Nestlé Waters North America decided to build a bottled-water plant in rural Wisconsin. Some local residents embraced the proposal because it seemed to represent economic development without environmental damage. "When you look at the different types of industry," remarked one real estate broker, "you can't get one much cleaner. There is no pollution, no noise." Others welcomed it because of the jobs that would be created, paying between $10.00 and $18.00 per hour, in an area sorely in need of an infusion of revenue and job opportunities. But the proposal alarmed environmentalists, who feared that pumping groundwater from a well located next to a small spring that flows naturally into the Mecan River would harm the river itself, a blue-ribbon trout stream.

The consumption of bottled water in the United States jumped 1,300 percent between 1978 and 2001. Bottled water has become a cultural phenomenon—a ubiquitous presence from gyms to movie theaters to classrooms. Bottled water has become Americans' third most popular beverage, behind only alcohol and carbonated drinks. The spurt in bottled-water sales from 2.5 billion dollars in 1991 to 7.7 billion dollars in 2002 has created enormous marketing opportunities because the retail markup for bottled water is extraordinary: The better-known brands of springwater fetch between $4.50 and $7.50 per gallon. Bottled water has a higher retail value than milk, oil, gasoline, or, paradoxically, many commodities made with water, such as Coca-Cola.

Beginning in the 1950s, the state of Wisconsin targeted the Mecan River for protection and since then has acquired over 6,000 acres of land on the river and its tributaries. Historically one of Wisconsin's most popular trout streams, the Mecan River sustains large populations of wild brown, brook, and rainbow trout. Nestlé's proposed pumping from the spring was a threat to the Mecan River because any reduction in the flow of the spring would diminish the flow in the river. Reducing its flow by as little as one cubic foot per second (7.5 gallons) would increase the river's temperature and impair fish spawning and larval rearing.

We know from the science of hydrology that pumping would have reduced the spring's flow. Nestlé planned to pump water from a well located only 60 feet away from the spring. The flow in this small spring ranges between 1,350 and 2,250 gallons per minute. The company wanted to pump 500 gallons per minute every hour of every day in the year, which amounts to 263 million gallons per year. The pumping from the well would have intercepted water beneath the surface of the Earth that is moving slowly toward the point where the spring emerges from the ground. As a consequence of the pumping, less water would have emerged from the spring and, in turn, less water would have flowed into the Mecan River. The pumping would have had catastrophic consequences.

Nestlé could have obtained water with a similar chemical content and potentially not degraded the river had it located its well as little as a mile away from the spring, but was reluctant to do so because it couldn't have labeled this water as "springwater." For marketing reasons, Nestlé has apparently determined that the term "springwater" has greater cachet with the American public than "artesian," "natural," "filtered," or "mineral" water. In order to sell "springwater," U.S. Food and Drug Administration rules require that the water come from a well located next to a spring. The FDA rules create a perverse, though unintended, incentive to harm the environment by pumping groundwater from a well so close to a spring that it reduces the spring's flow.

In Wisconsin, local residents quickly organized against Nestlé. Jon Steinhaus, co-chair of Waterkeepers of Wisconsin, proclaimed, "The springwater issue has struck a nerve like no other. This isn't a local issue. It is a state and national issue." Yet as local opposition to Nestlé's proposal grew, the state of Wisconsin found itself with few ways to prevent Nestlé from constructing the plant. Although

Wisconsin law required Nestlé to obtain a permit from the Department of Natural Resources, the department could deny the permit only if the well would interfere with a municipal water supply—an irrelevant issue in a rural area. The department had no choice but to grant Nestlé a permit. Environmental groups immediately filed lawsuits challenging the decision, but before these lawsuits were resolved, Nestlé moved on to the state of Michigan.

Michigan found itself in the same position as Wisconsin. An aide to Michigan's governor cautioned, "Michigan won't just be giving away the water; it will be paying a private and foreign-owned firm to take it away. If it were trees, natural gas, minerals, oil, or even sand, they would compensate the state." Despite this warning, the state granted Nestlé a permit, and construction of the bottling plant began in August 2001. Michigan had little choice. Under Michigan law, the Michigan Department of Environmental Quality could assess only the quality of the water that Nestlé would bottle, not the impact on the environment from the quantity of water that Nestlé would pump. In both Wisconsin and Michigan, state law required Nestlé to obtain a permit, but the standards for issuing the permits were so lax that the state agencies were unable to deny the permits.

Pumping for bottled water varies dramatically from most other water uses. When farmers or cities use water, they generate either return flow from agricultural runoff or effluent from a municipal water-treatment plant. Both return flow and effluent can be reused. In contrast, bottling water for sale is entirely for consumption. The water that goes into the bottles leaves the region for consumers in other cities and states.

The bottled-water controversy raises a serious issue of public policy: Should a state allow a private company to obtain control over a natural resource, such as water? For some natural resources, economics and history provide the answer. Mining oil, for example, requires an enormous investment of time, effort, and money. And even then there is no assurance that oil will be found in sufficient quantity to make the effort financially worthwhile. Hence, it makes some sense to reward those who risk labor and capital; otherwise people will be reluctant to take the gamble. But pumping springwater is a different matter altogether. The spring makes its presence known by bubbling to the surface. The bottler merely needs to conduct water-quality tests, construct a pipeline and a bottling facility, and bottle the water. It is difficult to justify windfall profits when a company has not underwritten the kind of risky investment required to find oil, and when the pumping either threatens the water supply of others or harms the environment.

Companies like Nestlé have an economic incentive to maximize their profit by selling water from a common resource—the aquifer. The company need not pay the costs of whatever environmental degradation occurs. Instead, it transfers these costs, what economists call externalities, to neighboring landowners and to society at large. These costs do not show up on the company's balance sheet. They never show up on a tax bill, on a monthly statement, or as an appropriation item. Instead, they appear as costs to the environment, for which we all must pay: degraded rivers, endangered species, depleted springs, dying trees, lost wetlands, ruined fisheries, altered flora, and threatened fauna.

The story of Nestlé's activities therefore raises vital questions: Who owns water? Should the government regulate its use? And, if the government does not, does that lead to systematic overuse?

The answer can be found in the history of water law in the United States. If we understand that history, we will understand how we arrived at this critical juncture and what we can do about it.

In the United States, water is both a public resource and a private property right, such as the law recognizes in land. But water is quite different from land: It moves, is reused, and is essential to the very existence of human life. The law historically has recognized water as a commodity—something to be used for economic development. Yet a water right is not an absolute right. There is a public interest component to all water rights in the United States. A right in water is a right to *use* the water, not a right of absolute ownership. Thus, rights in water differ fundamentally from rights in real estate, money, or jewels.

History accounts for this unique blend of public and private in water law. In the eastern United States, the early colonists borrowed the English system of riparian water rights, which emphasizes proximity. An owner of land abutting a lake or river had a right, by virtue of mere ownership of the real estate, to make use of the water in the lake or river. The right was shared with all other property owners on the lake or river. In the 19th century, riparian principles enabled the industrial revolution to flourish as New England factories harnessed the power of rivers. The legal structure of riparian rights has remained in effect in the eastern United States.

In the American West, courts developed a very different doctrine known as "prior appropriation," the essence of which is "first-in-time is first-in-right." Given the dearth of rivers in the West, miners and farmers were reluctant to undertake the considerable effort required to divert water from a river to their mines or fields (often several miles) without some assurance that they would be rewarded with a consistent and reliable supply of water. The prior appropriation doctrine encouraged development by rewarding the earliest diverters with rights to as much water as needed for any beneficial purpose. The courts liberally interpreted beneficial use to sanction the diversion of water through earthen (unlined) ditches for flood irrigation (notoriously inefficient) to grow water-guzzling but low-value crops, such as alfalfa. This doctrine still governs the uses of surface water in every western state (except California, which combines both riparian and prior appropriation rules).

This terribly inefficient system encouraged appropriators to divert as much water as possible, ignored the economic value of the activity for which the water was diverted, rewarded economic speculation, and created an incentive to hoard the resource because the appropriator was not required to pay. The government essentially gave away water to anyone who could use it. By recognizing rights to a specific quantity of water (whatever could be put to beneficial use), the prior appropriation doctrine transformed water into a commodity, like gold or timber. A public resource thus became private property.

The prior appropriation doctrine did insist that the water not be "wasted;" otherwise the water right would be forfeited or abandoned. To modern ears, however, the doctrine's conception of waste has a curious ring.

In 1926, Herbert Hoover expressed the economic and philosophical attitude of his day toward natural resources in general and water in particular. He put it this way: "True conservation of water is not the prevention of its use. Every drop of water that runs to the sea without yielding its full commercial returns to the nation is an economic waste."

Then, to waste water was to fail to *use* the water, as opposed to fail to *conserve* the water. Over time, as western farmers irrigated additional lands with surface water, more and more water was diverted from rivers—eventually drying up many. Until recently, the dewatering of a river seemed a small price to pay for the benefits of economic development. Early settlers were not concerned with environmental protection, ecosystem management, or riparian habitat. Nature was to be explored, conquered, and tamed.

To understand how Nestlé could obtain rights to water for its bottled-water operations, it is necessary to understand that groundwater use, unlike surface water use, is largely unregulated to this day. In the 19th century when American courts developed groundwater law, the science of hydrology was in its infancy. The principles by which water moved beneath the ground were not well known. Given this uncertainty, American courts essentially shrugged their shoulders and said: "If you can get the water out of the ground, it is yours." Since then the science of hydrology has matured, and we understand how groundwater moves. Alas, the legal system has not kept pace, and as a consequence the legal rules fail to conform with physical reality. Most states have two different sets of rules, one for surface water and another for groundwater.

When American courts developed these groundwater rules in the 19th century, the judges believed that groundwater was an inexhaustible resource. Now we know better. Groundwater comes from aquifers—geologic formations in which water has collected over thousands of years. Think of an aquifer as a giant milkshake glass and each well as a straw in the glass. Most states permit a limitless number of straws to be put into the single glass.

The recent drought caused U.S. cities, mines, farmers, and individual homeowners to scramble in search of new water supplies. Most often groundwater was identified as the solution to the problem of water shortages. Groundwater pumping in the United States has increased dramatically in recent decades. For domestic purposes alone, groundwater use jumped from 8 billion gallons per day in 1965 to approximately 18.5 in 1995, the most recent year for which federal statistics have been compiled. This is equivalent to 65 gallons *per day* for every man, woman, and child in the country. And domestic consumption is only a small fraction of the country's total groundwater use—a staggering 28 *trillion* gallons in 1995. Farmers used two-thirds of that to irrigate crops, and the mining industry pumped approximately 770 billion gallons. Groundwater use has increased so sharply that even in 1995 it constituted more than 25 percent of the nation's water supply and provided drinking water for more than half of the country's population.

The country cannot sustain the current levels of ground-water use, never mind the increases that are expected over the next two decades, as the U.S. population increases and sources of surface water, already scarce, become increasingly unavailable for human use. Our enormous expansion of groundwater pumping since the 1940s—a blink of an eye in geologic time—has caused serious environmental problems. Overdrafting, or the "mining" of groundwater, raises the specter of running out of water altogether. In some areas of the country, water table levels are dropping, requiring the drilling of deeper wells, often at considerable expense. Pumping from lower depths will increase costs, because it will require substantially more energy to lift the water. And water pumped from lower levels is often of poorer quality because naturally occurring contaminants, such as arsenic, fluoride, and radon are more prevalent at deeper levels in the Earth, and the Earth's higher internal temperature at these levels dissolves more of these elements into solution. Along coastal areas, overdrafting may cause the intrusion of salt water into the aquifer, which ruins the water for human consumption. Groundwater pumping may also cause land subsidence, a phenomenon in which the land surface actually cracks open or drops, in some cases dramatically. Finally, groundwater pumping can have very serious consequences for the health of lakes, rivers, streams, springs, wetlands, and estuaries.

Allowing unlimited use of a common resource inevitably produces what biologist Garrett Hardin called "the tragedy of the commons." In the case of resources not owned by individuals, such as air, water, oceans, and wildlife, consumers who seek to maximize their individual welfare will simultaneously reduce social welfare. Examples of the tragedy of the commons include fouled air, polluted water, overgrazed public lands, clear-cut public forests, overharvested fisheries, and overhunted buffalo. Economists describe these activities as creating externalized costs, ones not absorbed by the individuals who engage in the activity but imposed instead on their neighbors or on society generally. As long as the resource is public and no barriers limit consumption, the possibility exists for individuals to decimate the common resource. For groundwater, the benefit from increased pumping—each new straw in the glass—goes entirely to the pumper, but the costs of environmental degradation are shared by all citizens who use the aquifer and by society at large.

The excessive pumping of aquifers has created an environmental catastrophe known to only a few scientists, a handful of water-management experts, and those unfortunate enough to have suffered the direct consequences. As groundwater use has increased, the pumping has caused rivers, springs, lakes, and wetlands to dry up, ground to collapse, wildlife, trees, and shrubs to die. In the Southwest, verdant rivers, such as the Santa Cruz in Tucson, have become desiccated sandboxes as cities pumped underground water until the surface water simply disappeared. Around Tampa Bay, Florida, groundwater pumping has turned lakes into mudflats and has cracked the foundations of homes. Outside Boston, the Ipswich River has gone dry in four of the last eight years. These illustrations offer a glimpse of the future, as operations such as Nestlé's cater to the voracious demand of a burgeoning population. Fresh water is becoming scarce, not just in the arid West, with its tradition of battling over water rights, but even in places we think of as relatively wet.

The need to regulate groundwater pumping is a matter of considerable urgency, because groundwater moves slowly and it may take years or even decades until groundwater pumping affects surface waters. The hidden tragedy and irremediable fact is that groundwater pumping that has occurred already will cause environmental damage in the future. But we can control future pumping. So let's consider how to reform the system.

To prevent the tragedy of the commons, we must break the cycle of unrestricted access to the common-pool resource (groundwater). The question is how to do so. Some advocates oppose recognizing private rights in water on the ground that water is a public resource. They resist any privatization of water resources. The notion of water as a public resource has an appealing ring in the abstract, but in the concrete, water-allocation decisions would be made by public officials (elected or appointed). That's our current system. Few would argue that the existing distribution of water through the decisions of public officials is efficient, rational, or equitable. Nor would many economists or political observers argue that legislative decisions are made strictly in the public interest—even assuming we could agree on a definition of "the public interest."

At the other end of the spectrum, some economists and free-market advocates yearn for an ideal world: water as private property. They argue that the only way to avoid the tragedy of the commons is to end limitless access to the common-pool resource and to create, as a substitute, a system of private property rights in water. A market in water rights would certainly encourage more efficient use of water. At the same time, those who worship the market must put their faith in egregious fictions, such as the assumption that consumers have perfect knowledge of all available choices. For water rights, in particular, the market is less than efficient because of what economists call transaction costs, those costs necessary to make the market work. It takes time and money to identify willing sellers of water, to establish the value of their water rights, to determine whether the water rights of third parties may encumber the sale, to negotiate the terms, and to assess whether the proposed contracts can be enforced.

Even more important is the fact that any market system has difficulty internalizing environmental costs. Economists expect, in a private property system, that a rational property owner will protect the environment on his or her property. But the holder of a water right—whether ground or surface water—has no incentive to protect rivers or streams on someone else's (or the government's) land. Therefore, creating private property rights in water will not eliminate the degradation of rivers and riparian habitat or prevent other environmental harm from groundwater pumping. A property right in water creates an incentive for landowners to protect the resource only to the extent necessary to assure them access to the full quantity of their rights. For groundwater pumpers, this incentive is quite modest because they will almost always be able to pump the full measure of their rights, regardless of how many other wells draw from the same aquifer. Over time, their collective action may draw down the water table, which will increase the cost of pumping, but probably not to such a degree that pumpers are prevented from obtaining all the water they want.

To control the impact of water use on the environment, a command-and-control model of government rules and regulations must be combined with the market forces of transferable rights and price incentives. The first step toward more efficient water use is to quantify the rights of existing users and to make those rights transferable. If they can be transferred, they become valuable. And by protecting existing users, the states can break free of the relentless cycle of increasing use by placing restrictions on individual freedom to drill *new* wells.

States need to foster a market in water rights by allowing rights to be easily transferred from existing users to newcomers. Water markets involve voluntary decisions made by willing buyers and sellers. Much water use in the United States currently sustains low-value economic activity, such as growing alfalfa for cattle feed. A water-rights market would help to shift water from low-value uses to higher-value ones. A farmer growing alfalfa, for example, might then choose to transfer (sell) some of his water to a developer or municipality. The value of the water right would increase as the use for the water generated greater economic benefits.

Yet market forces alone are inadequate to protect our environment. States should also craft water conservation standards that require all users to make more efficient use of water resources. And to eliminate the tragedy of the commons, states must get tough on unregulated groundwater pumping. In particular, states should reexamine permissive rules that allow corporations, such as Nestlé, to tap into a resource that provides the water supply for a community or that sustains critical environmental habitat. It makes no sense for states to continue to give away their water.

Local governments should also use financial incentives as a significant part of water policy. To put it quite simply, we are not paying the true cost of water. When homeowners or businesses receive a monthly water bill from a city's water department or a private water company, that bill usually includes only the extraction costs of drilling the wells, the energy costs of pumping the water, the infrastructure costs of the distribution and storage system, and the administrative costs of the water department or company. Water rates, with rare exceptions, do *not* include a commodity charge for the water. The water itself is free! To illustrate the absurdity of this, imagine Texaco charging a customer at the pump only the cost of the electricity to pump the gas.

Even though water is a scarce commodity, in the sense that unchecked demand can easily exceed available supply, most Americans have not yet faced the condition that economists call *scarcity*, which occurs when people alter their consumption patterns in response to price increases. Habits of water use will not change until the cost of water rises sufficiently to force an alteration. Therefore, we must increase water rates so that all users pay the *replacement* value of the water, which is not just the cost of drilling a new well, but also the cost of retiring an existing user's well.

Economists agree that significant price increases would create incentives for all users to conserve. Each farmer, homeowner, business, or industrial user could then decide which uses of water to continue and which to curtail. Rate increases would encourage the elimination of marginal economic activities and the movement of water toward more productive uses. An increase in rates might stimulate new technologies and water-harvesting efforts. It would certainly encourage greater use of effluents, a by-product that can be employed for uses such as outdoor watering.

At the same time, persons of fixed or modest income should be sheltered from any significant increase in water rates for basic domestic needs. Residential use that exceeds a certain threshold—particularly during the summer as contrasted with the winter—usually reflects water use associated with discretionary purposes, such as swimming pools or lush outdoor landscaping, which need not be protected. Water rights ought to target such discretionary uses by imposing graduated, increasing block rates for consumption above the threshold requirement for basic human needs.

Through these reforms, we can break the relentless cycle of overuse and begin to use our water resources more wisely. Change will not come easily or quickly. However, if we succeed, there is reason to be optimistic because nature has enormous regenerative capacity. And there is incentive to try. The future of our springs, rivers, lakes, and wetlands depends on it.

THE WORLD'S WATER:

A HUMAN RIGHT OR A CORPORATE GOOD?

Maude Barlow

Augusts 29, 2002, in Orange Farm, South Africa, is a hot, dusty day. The air is filled with the acrid smell of burning garbage and tires. Two buses pull up at the same time in this impoverished township near Johannesburg. The World Summit on Sustainable Development (WSSD) has brought thousands of people from around the world to assess the progress on the environmental front since the first Earth Summit held in Rio ten years before. The event has become mired in controversy, as civil society groups accuse transnational water companies of taking over the summit for their own purposes, and World Bank and World Trade Organization officials move in to assure their agendas will not be derailed by the proceedings. Police have already fired stun grenades into a peaceful march against water privatization and water cutoffs in the townships. Tempers are running high.

Seventy-five anti-privatization activists from Africa and around the world emerge from an old yellow school bus that has seen better days. From another, a big, new, double-decker BMW, descend dozens of executives in expensive suits from Suez, the giant French water company, as well as a number of European Union delegates to the summit. Both groups are drawn here by a string of high-tech water meters newly installed outside a row of tar-paper shacks and pit latrines. The Suez executives, whose company built Orange Farm's water system, are here to show off their work to the European politicians. They are keen to get more World Bank contracts such as this one and have come to the WSSD to promote water privatization to the delegates. The activists are deeply opposed to for-profit water services in desperately poor communities such as Orange Farm and have come to see for themselves how the water meters are used to prevent the locals from getting clean water.

Small barefoot children play in the dust. The activists and the Suez executives start to talk and realize that they are on opposite sides of the great divide in the world of water. Voices are raised and soon local residents are shouting at the retreating backs of the water executives running for the safety of their bus. Furious locals follow right onto the buses, excoriating Suez for bringing hardship, disease, and death into Orange Farm with their water meters. Finally, the big BMW bus careers off to the safety of the open highway soundtracked by the shouting of hundreds of villagers.

Orange Farm on that August day was a microcosm of a ferocious fight being waged in communities all over the world around the crucial question of access to water. When apartheid was defeated in 1993 and the new government of Nelson Mandela was sworn in the next year, South Africa became a role model for the world by guaranteeing water for all in its constitution. The government began the long process of building water-delivery systems to millions of township residents living without running water. But under the influence of the World Bank, South Africa privatized many of its water services. Johannesburg turned its system over to Suez, which began the process of installing state-of-the-art meters outside of every home about to receive its constitutionally guaranteed allotment of water. This was to ensure compliance with the new "cost-recovery" program, which makes water availability dependent on a company's ability to recover its full cost of delivery including profit for its investors. Impoverished South Africans, unable to afford to feed the meters, turned back to their little rivers of cholera for water supplies, and the government has cut off water services to over ten million people since the introduction of new programs since 1996. Ninety percent of the wastewater of developing nations is discharged untreated into local waterways. Without access to government-delivered clean water, millions of people are ill. More than 120,000 people in Kwazulu-Natal province became ill with cholera recently when water and sanitation services were discontinued for nonpayment. This situation, being echoed in developing countries around the world, gives new meaning to the line "water, water, everywhere and not a drop to drink."

Scarcity seemed to sneak up on us. Until the last decade the study of fresh water was left to highly specialized groups of experts—hydrologists, engineers, scientists, city planners, weather forecasters, and others with a niche interest in what so many of us still take for granted. Many in the First World knew about the condition of water in the developing world, but this was seen as an issue of poverty, poor sanitation, and injustice, not as a consequence of water shortages per se. Now, however, we know that a legacy of factory farming, flood irrigation, the construction of massive dams, toxic dumping, wetlands and forest destruction, and urban and industrial pollution has damaged the Earth's surface water so badly that we are now mining underground water reserves far faster than nature can replenish them.

Unlimited growth is the driving mantra of our time. And nation-states are ruthlessly exploiting water supplies to stay competitive, abandoning natural resources protection and privatizing their ecological commons. Governments around the world are abdicating the responsibility to protect the natural resources in their territory, giving authority to private companies involved in resource extraction. Developing world governments are actually selling off whole river systems to foreign companies to relieve their debt; even wealthy countries like Canada give massive water licenses to oil companies who use ancient aquifer water to pump oil at fire-sale prices.

Both the World Bank and the United Nations state that water is a "human need" not a "human right." The difference in interpretation is subtle, yet fundamental. There are many ways to supply a human need. A human right cannot be sold or traded.[1]

A handful of transnational corporations are aggressively taking over the management of public water services in countries around the world, dramatically raising the price of water for local residents. The decline in freshwater supplies and standards has created a wonderful venture opportunity for water corporations and their investors. The agenda is clear: Water should be treated like any other tradable good, with its use determined by the principles of profit.

There are ten major corporate players now delivering freshwater services for profit. Between them, the three largest—Suez and Vivendi Environment of France and RWE-AG of Germany—deliver water and wastewater services to almost 300 million customers in over 100 countries. Their growth is exponential; a decade ago, they served around 51 million people in just 12 countries. At the moment, private players control less than 10 percent of the world's water systems but, at their current rate of expansion, within the next ten years the top three alone could have control of over 70 percent of water systems in North American and Europe.[2]

But there are other players too, such as Bouygues SAUR, Thames Water (owned by RWE), and Bechtel-United Utilities. Chemical giant Monsanto sees the growing water crisis as an opportunity and is heavily investing in what it sees as a potential multibillion-dollar business. The company plans to penetrate markets in India and Mexico and declares openly on its Web site, "There are markets in which there are predictable sustainability challenges and therefore opportunities to create business value."

The revenue growth of the big three has kept pace. Vivendi earned just five billion dollars (U.S.) a decade ago in its water-related revenues; by 2002 that amount had increased to over 12 billion dollars. RWE, which moved into the world market with its acquisition of Britain's Thames Water, increased its water revenues a whopping 9,786 percent in ten years. All three are among the top 100 corporations in the world; together their annual revenues in 2001 were almost 160 billion dollars and growing at 10 percent a year—outpacing the economies of many of the countries in which they operate. They also employ more staff than most governments: As of 2001, Vivendi Environment employs 295,000 worldwide; Suez employs 188,000.

The companies are creating sophisticated lobbying groups to encourage the passage of legislation friendly to their interests. In France, the big two have long had close political ties with national and local governments. In Washington, they have secured beneficial tax law changes and are working to persuade Congress to pass laws that would force cash-strapped municipalities to consider privatization of their water systems in exchange for federal grants and loans. The United States alone is expected to spend one trillion dollars in the next three decades to upgrade aging waterworks. Financial fund managers are taking note of the expanding water market. Switzerland's second oldest bank, the Pictet Bank, recently started its Global Water Fund in the U.S. after launching a similar one in Europe in 2000. The bank offers a basket of water companies and predicts that by 2015, 75 percent of Europe's water utilities will be privatized.

The performance of these companies in Europe and the developing world has been well documented: huge profits, higher prices for water, cutoffs to customers who cannot pay, reduced water quality, bribery, and corruption.

One of the more celebrated cases of the latter involves Suez; after an investigation into allegations of corruption, a team of magistrates in Grenoble France concluded that the city's water service had been privatized in 1989 in exchange for donations totaling 19 million francs, made by the company to the election campaign of the city's mayor, Alain Caigon. In 1996, both Caigon (who by then was minister of communications in the government of France) and Jean-Jacques Prompsey (who by then was chief executive of Suez's international water management division) were convicted of accepting/paying bribes and sentenced to time in prison. Another case of bribery had to do with Vivendi and the city of Angouleme in France. In 1997, Jean-Michel Boucheron, former mayor (and later a junior cabinet minister in the French government) was convicted and sentenced to two years in jail for taking bribes from companies that were bidding for public service concessions in Angouleme.

In July 2002, Suez terminated one of the largest private water concessions in the world. Suez ended its 30-year contract to provide water and sewerage services to the city of Buenos Aires, which served a population of ten million people, when the Argentine financial crisis turned company profits into losses. The Buenos Aires privatization deal, consummated in 1993, had been widely lauded by the World Bank, the Argentine government, and the water industry as an international success story.

According to a recent report published by Public Citizen: "During the first eight years of the contract, weak regulatory practices and contract renegotiations that eliminated corporate risk enabled the Suez subsidiary, Aguas Argentinas S.A., to earn a 19 percent profit rate on its average net worth." Water rates, which the company said would be reduced by 27 percent, actually rose 20 percent. To counter union resistance to the price increases, the company gave the workers 10 percent ownership. In exchange, the union consented to a 50 percent staff reduction. Then, Aguas Argentinas reneged on its contractual obligations to build a new sewage treatment plant; now, more than 95 percent of the city's sewage is dumped directly into the Río de la Plata.[3]

Local citizens were outraged. Hundreds of thousands signed a plebiscite to force the water company to leave. Now similar citizen-led plebiscites are being held in Rosario and Santa Fe. Working from tiny offices or homes, citizens are turning the tide on water privatization in Argentina. They cite these facts: The companies pay no taxes, refuse to comply with their original contracts, consistently raise prices so that many Argentinians can no longer afford water, charge inflated rates of interest, cut environmental corners resulting in historic levels of water toxicity, and cut services to pensioners, the unemployed, and schools.

A few years earlier, an equally disturbing situation emerged on the other side of the globe, this time with Vivendi and Thames Water. Fifteen months after Adelaide, Australia, signed a contract in 1995 turning over its waterworks to a consortium controlled by Thames Water and Vivendi, the city was engulfed by a powerful sewage smell, which became known as "the big pong" (stench). An independent investigation by the University of Queensland found that the consortium's drive to minimize costs had caused it to cut corners on equipment and monitoring, which led to the fouling of a major holding lagoon. This problem came on top of huge rate hikes—59 percent in seven years—and layoffs of 48 percent of the city's water staff.

In another high-profile case, elevated levels of the parasites *Cryptosporidium* and *Giardia* forced the residents of Sydney to boil drinking water during the winter of 1998. An independent government review laid the blame at the feet of Australian Water Services, a consortium of Suez and Australian financial interests, citing the company's cost-cutting measures. Christopher Shell of the University of New South Wales said that the private water plant was "geared to operate as cheaply as possible. Finance was the driver, not productivity."

Another privatization disaster story emerged in early 2003 when the largest water privatization in the United States was overturned amid a growing chorus of dismay. In 1999, Atlanta, Georgia, contracted with United Water (a Suez subsidiary) to run the city's water system for 20 years. City officials cited service that was poor, unresponsive and fraught with breakdowns," including an epidemic of water main breaks and regular "boil-only" alerts caused by brown water pouring from city taps. Mayor Shirley Franklin said that the city would once again run its own water to ensure it is "in safe hands."

The chorus of dismay erupted into an actual uprising in Cochabamba, Bolivia, when Bechtel set up a subsidiary, Aguas del Tunari, which immediately raised the price of water beyond the reach of the vast majority of the population. The contract even gave the company the right to charge people for the water they took from their own wells and collected in rain barrels. In fact, Bechtel and the British-led consortium of investors put up less than $20,000 of up-front capital for a water system worth millions. Consumers endured rate increases while the company was expected to earn an annual income of 58 million dollars. A general strike was called by a five-foot, slightly built machinist named Oscar Olivera, who immediately came under death threats from the military. Thousands of citizens took to the streets in a confrontation with the army that left many injured and a 17-year-old dead. Bechtel was forced out, and the water services in Cochabamba are now run by a citizen-controlled non-profit company.

There was more push-back from Ghana's citizens when they recently stopped a plan for water privatization as the government announced a 95 percent hike in water fees—in a country where 70 percent of the people earn less than a dollar a day. And in Puerto Rico it was the government, not the citizens, who issued a strongly worded report in 1999 against a Vivendi subsidiary, Compania de Aguas, for failing to adequately maintain and repair the state's aqueducts and sewers. In 2001, the government issued another warning to the company, citing 3,181 deficiencies in the administration, operation, and maintenance of the water infrastructure.

These private water companies could not have expanded without the protection of a number of powerful institutions with which they work closely. The main source of financing of private water services in the developing world is the International Monetary Fund (IMF), which often demands that a debtor country privatize its water services in order to obtain debt relief. Encouraging poor countries to privatize their water is part of a process called structural adjustment that has been used to force the developing nations to adopt market-based economic policies favored by the powerful governments and corporations of industrialized countries. The IMF and the World Bank have compelled over 80 countries to weaken their tools of national sovereignty by deeply cutting public spending, deregulating state enterprises such as transportation and energy, and dismantling protections for domestic industry. In this way, big transnational corporations of North America, Europe, and Japan have gained access to the markets and resources of the developing nations. A top U.S. Treasury official once boasted to Congress that for every dollar the U.S. contributes to the World Bank, American corporations receive $1.30 back in contracts.

The World Bank serves the interests of water companies through the International Bank for Reconstruction and Development, which provides loans to governments and can impose conditions in exchange for money, and the International Finance Corporation, which provides direct capital funding. Lending about 20 billion dollars to water-supply projects over the past decade, the World Bank has been the principal financer of privatization. A year-long study by the International Consortium of Investigative Journalists, a project of the Washington-based Center for Public Integrity, released in February 2003, found that the majority of World Bank loans for water in the past five years have required the conversion of public systems to private as a condition for the transaction.

Further, the World Bank has set the stage for some of the worst privatizations on record. In South Africa, it helped persuade local councils not only to hire private water companies but also to introduce a "credible threat of cutting service" that led to cut-offs for millions of poor. In Bolivia, the Bank's advice led to a nationwide uprising in which a 17-year-old was killed and many were injured in clashes with the army.

Not content to work one on one, the water companies and the World Bank have joined forces through the United Nations to create a set of international think tanks, lobby groups, advisory commissions, and forums that have come to dominate the water debate and set the stage for a private future for water. The most powerful is the World Water Council (WWC), formed in 1996, a policy think tank whose main task is to promote privatization with government decision-makers. Representatives of the global water corporations are strategically placed at the top levels of the WWC; one of its three founding members is Rene Coulomb, a former Suez vice president.

Every three years the WWC organizes a World Water Forum (WWF), which has become a major platform for the water corporations. The forum has all the trappings of an official United Nations conference, including a ministerial meeting. At both the second WWF in the Netherlands in March 2000 and the third in Kyoto, Japan, in March 2003 (attended by over 8,000 people), water corporations and World Bank officials succeeded in stopping a campaign to get governments to declare water a human right, opting for the more corporate-friendly language of a "human need." Government delegates then take this language back to their own countries, where it profoundly affects all areas of water policy. In Kyoto, a well-organized group of anti-privatization civil society activists challenged the WWC; the rallying cry of "no consensus" on water privatization was prominently picked up by the international media.

These corporations and their powerful institutional associations—including the U.S. Coalition of Service Industries and the European Forum on Services—also work closely with the World Trade Organization (WTO) and regional trade institutions to further the liberalization of national laws in relationship to water. The WTO is mandated to remove tariff and nontariff barriers to the free flow of goods, including water, across national borders and is currently negotiating free trade in water through its services negotiations called the General Agreement on Trade in Services (GATS). On behalf of its powerful private sector, the European Union is requesting that all countries put their water services on the table under the heading of "environmental services."

At the WTO Ministerial in Doha, Qatar, in December 2001, Europe added a last-minute provision to the deal that required all member countries to give up "tariff and nontariff" barriers—which could include environmental regulation or laws to keep water delivery in public hands—to environmental services, including water. The water corporations even attended the World Summit on Sustainable Development in Johannesburg, South Africa, in August 2002, where they launched a "new" strategy for the delivery of efficient water and sanitation services to the world's poor based on public-private partnerships—the model preferred by the WTO.

The North American Free Trade Agreement and almost 2,000 Bilateral Investment Agreements (BITs) contain an "investor-state" provision that allows corporations to sue governments who introduce laws "unfriendly" to their interests. Already, a California company is suing the government of Canada for ten billion dollars because the province of British Columbia banned the export of water for commercial purposes. And Bechtel is using a BIT to sue Bolivia for 25 million dollars because the uprising forced the company to leave the country. In a blow to democracy, the World Bank's International Center for the Settlement of Investment Disputes, which is hearing the case, ruled in February 2003 that it would not allow the public or media to participate in or even witness the proceedings. If the WTO has its way, there will one day be similar investment provisions in the GATS as well.

This is a crucial moment. The decisions we make now about the ownership of water will determine who will have access to this dwindling resource. European water activist Ricardo Petrella says that a kind of "global high command" for water has been building up in the past decade. Faster than most realize, water is becoming a cartel to be controlled by a small but powerful global elite. The World Bank has stated, "One way or another, water will soon be moved around the world as oil is now." If this is allowed to continue, there may come a time in the not-too-distant future when all decisions regarding water will center on commercial, not environmental or social justice, considerations.

The answer to the world's growing water crisis lies on the twin foundations of conservation and equity. Even the most conscientious of private companies cannot run a business on those ethics. There are some areas of life that should be marked a part of "the commons" and set aside from the rules of the marketplace.

Water is one of them. Water belongs to the Earth and all species and is a fundamental human right. No one has the right to appropriate it for private profit. Water must be declared a public trust, and all governments must enact legislation to protect the freshwater resources in their territories. Until that time, expect more showdowns like Orange Farm. And expect them to get more violent. Expect also the rise of a powerful civil society movement to challenge the lords of water. No one gave the world's water to them. People and nature will take it back.

THREE RIVERS

Marq de Villiers

Cui Wei Yan, who lives in poverty in a single-room cave in northern Shaanxi Province with his elderly wife, Zhang Zhen Lian, their daughter, and grandson, doesn't know it, but the bigwigs in Beijing are working to solve his water problems. Not through anything so mundane as laying pipe to the nearby village but through a project grand enough, in its way, to match even that *folie de grandeur,* the Great Wall of China. Cui Wei Yan's political masters plan to recreate agriculture and water-hungry industry in the arid north, among the rapidly advancing dunes on the fringes of the Gobi, and on the great plains around Beijing, where the water tables have been dropping more than a meter a year for the past decade. They plan to do this by essentially reengineering the entire country, by diverting massive amounts of water from the sodden south to the parched north in a series of canals, conduits, reservoirs, and pipes, with a price tag somewhere around 58 billion dollars (U.S.).

It will be, by far, the largest civil engineering project on the planet. It may never get finished. And it might not work if it does.

Meanwhile Mr. Cui, who is 78 years old and has lived in the same cave all his life, as his father did before him and his grandfather before that, sets out every morning after sunup with two buckets on a yoke across his shoulders, to fetch the family's daily ration of water. He trudges up the steep hillside, heading for the cistern that the local authorities have set into the hillside a kilometer away. He drops his buckets into the cistern on a rope and hauls out the water. It is not exactly clean—bits of grass and debris are floating in it—but then neither are his buckets. The operation takes him about 45 minutes, longer, as he admits, than it used to. Back at the cave, he tips some of the water into the small tin basin the whole family uses for washing, and the rest into a rank barrel, from which cooking water will be drawn.

"We have a saying," said Mr. Cui, who is full of sayings and impish smiles, "that we don't wash our faces in the morning—we wash our eyes. We don't have enough water for the whole face."

Earlier he had said of his way of life: "We bathe three times in our lives: when we are born, when we marry, and when we die."

The peasant farmers of Shandong Province on their new private plots were the first to suffer. In the early 1990s, the level of water in their wells began to drop. They weren't aware of it yet, for Beijing had said nothing, but the water tables were dropping all over northern and northeastern China. The peasant farmers knew only that there was less water than there had been. In 1994, some of the wells went dry, and the following year hundreds more. All over the region, farmers and their families took time from cultivation to dig. They pushed the wells down another meter, two more meters, and found water. In 1996, their wells dried up again. The water tables on the North China Plain had dropped more than four meters in three years, and no one knew where it would end. For several years, at a time when water demands were soaring, rainfall had been meager and rivers lower than usual. Extractions from river systems had historically been for agriculture, but China's astonishing economic boom, and its expanding industries and cities, were placing massive demands on finite water systems. China's own figures say that between 1983 and 1990 the number of cities short of water tripled to 300, almost half the cities in the country; those whose problem was described as "serious" rose from 40 to 100. By the year 2000, the Chinese said in 1998, municipal Beijing would suffer a daily water shortfall of 500,000 cubic meters, but it reached that dismal target before 1999 had arrived.

By 2002 the drought, and the shortages in the north, had gotten worse. In Shandong, villagers who had traditionally drawn water from a leaking reservoir rioted when workmen began to repair the leaks. In the northeastern city of Dalian, close to the Outer

Mongolia border, water was so scarce that it was being rationed for domestic users, and hundreds of bathhouses were closed. Even in the prosperous southern province of Guangdong, almost 100 reservoirs had dried up and rivers were reduced to trickles.

Recognition that a crisis is at hand is fairly recent. The region's water supply first began to seem fragile only two decades ago, and it is now only a few years since hydrologists and ecologists have turned their attention to the problem. Late in his life, Henry Kendall, Nobel Prize-winning Harvard physicist and eminent scholar, turned his formidable intelligence to the question of world food supplies, which he believed was the critical issue for the next few decades. Lester Brown's controversial wake-up call *Who Will Feed China?* tracked the statistics and forecast that severe water shortages would force China to import food.

But in practice, much of the problem is mismanagement, or what Vaclav Smil, a researcher at the University of Manitoba, calls "Maoist stupidities." These include establishing water-thirsty industries in dry northern cities like Beijing, badly planned dams, poorly managed rivers, and attempts to grow unsuitable crops requiring irrigation in the driest parts of the country. In northern Shaanxi, for example, an arid place where dunes are already beginning to roll over remnants of the Great Wall, they continue to grow rice in the riverbeds. China has barely experimented with more efficient water-delivery systems; it badly needs to replace open irrigation ditches with sprinkler systems and drip agriculture. The first step should be to charge a fee for water. "Right now farmers basically get their water for free," Brian Halweil, a WorldWatch staffer, points out. "If there were even a marginal, symbolic charge, it would spur all sorts of conservation efforts." But even in China, removing subsidies is politically risky; the authorities don't want to reopen the social unrest that occurred during the Three Gorges forced relocations, when riots by expropriated workers and peasants spread alarm through the communist hierarchy.

Why is China running out of water? The answer is the same as for the rest of the world: It isn't running out. It's only running out in places where it's needed most. The problem is one of allocation, supply, and management.

In the summer of 1998, one of the wettest on record, water was certainly not running out in the humid south. The Yangtze, swollen by sustained downpours, reached its highest level since 1954 and killed more than 2,000 people in its rampages across the lower valley.

In 2002, another 650 people drowned in a flood in Changsha in Hunan Province. It took an army of soldiers and civilians, nearly 900,000 of them, to pile sandbags on the shores of the dangerously swollen Dongting Lake, as the Yangtze flood crest raced toward it. If the dam, China's second largest, had ruptured, water would have swept across a flat plain that was home to ten million farmers. Two cities, Changsha and Wuhan, with a combined population of seven million, would have been at risk. Water levels were three meters above the norm.

The floods illustrate China's central water dilemma, which is that the country has enough water, but it is in the wrong place at the wrong times and in the wrong amounts. Three-quarters of the water is in the south, and three-quarters of the farming is in the north and northeast. The south includes the Yangtze, and about 700 million people. The much drier north, inhabited by some 500 million people, includes the Yellow, Liao, Hai, and Huai Rivers. All the northern rivers are stretched to the limit, and already the water supply for 200 million people is assured only through unsustainable mining of groundwater. The Yellow River, the "cradle of Chinese civilization," already dries up in bad years before it reaches the sea. Development projects scheduled for its upper reaches will make matters considerably worse, including hydroelectric schemes and a canal to Mongolia.

The supply problem has been gravely compromised by the quality of the water that is still available. Almost 80 percent of the rivers contain water unfit for human consumption; there is a serious danger that irrigated crops in the worst areas might poison the population instead of nurturing it.

China has not always been forthcoming about this or any water matter, but for some decades there were strong signals that a crisis was anxiously predicted. In 1988, a new water law was passed, and the agencies responsible for water, soil conservation, and other regulations were consolidated in a bureaucratically superior Ministry of Water Resources. The ministry controls water policy formulation; strategic planning, including flood control, water pollution, and wastewater controls; economic regulation; and conflict arbitration. Sensibly, the subministries were organized by river basin, each responsible for a major river system. The next sublevel was the conservancy commissions, which governed tributaries. The new system was designed to resolve what the announcement delicately called the "conflicts and shortfalls" of the older system. That nothing had been done about the dikes and floodplains of the Yangtze by 1998 was not a reassuring sign that the new bureaucracy was any more flexible than the old. Political strategies hardly ever coincided neatly with basin boundaries, and it was difficult to get anything done.

But starting around 1999, the Chinese stopped pretending. One of the first signs was the sudden attention paid to the attempt to save the failing Baiyang Dian freshwater lake system, the largest in north China, stretching across the flat plains that lie to the south of Beijing. In the 1950s, the lakes of Baiyang Dian covered more than 310 square miles. Today, local officials say only 186 square miles remain underwater; Professor Liu Changming of the Chinese Academy of Sciences puts the figure closer to 44 square miles. What water remains is severely polluted. Nevertheless, there are concerted efforts in the national media and from Beijing to find remedies.

Early in 2002, the central authorities issued a "water classification zone table," dividing the country into some 13,000 water environment zones, classifying 5,737 rivers and 980 lakes and reservoirs as zones for natural protection, drinking, industrial and agricultural use, sightseeing, and entertainment. By midyear, Beijing was sending out weekly, and sometimes daily, bulletins that occasionally seemed to be verging on panic. The State Environmental Protection Administration reported: "The overall situation in China is grave." Pollution in all the seven major rivers was approaching catastrophe; acid rain was falling on 30 percent of the country; the East China and Bo Hai Seas were so polluted that fishing was threatened; China's deserts were expanding at about

3,000 square kilometers a year; there were major dust storms across northern cities that lasted 45 days from March to May. Zhu Jianqiu, the agency's vice minister, estimated that fully 90 percent of usable natural grasslands in China, with an aggregate area of 135 million hectares, were suffering from varying degrees of degradation. Statistics issued in Beijing declared that water shortages were already causing 15 billion dollars a year in lost industrial output. In May the same year, China's vice premier, Wen Jiabao, declared that fully one-third of China's entire landmass—and bear in mind this is the fourth largest country in the world—was facing what he called "severe land degradation" caused by water loss, soil erosion, overly saline soils, and accelerating desertification. Wen was talking candidly to the 12th International Soil Conservation Organization Conference in Beijing. He blamed the problems on a shopping list of causes: careless management, inadequate infrastructure, irresponsible agricultural initiatives, and— a prime cause—deforestation of the country.

Traveling up from the Yellow River Falls toward China's northern frontier, we passed a vast area of high hills deeply scored with erosional gullies. It was in one of those hills that Mr. Cui and his family lived in their one-room cave. Like much of China, all the hills were patterned with the parallel stripes of planting terraces. From the bottom of the gorges to the tips of the hills, and for as far as the eye could see, the countryside has been manicured for hundreds and even thousands of years by the busy work of millions of peasant farmers, until it sometimes appears that hardly a centimeter of the Chinese countryside has escaped. But on thousands of hillsides, the only plantings were of trees. The peasants had been told to no longer plant food crops. The constant irrigation of those hundreds of thousands of terraces had, in the end, exaggerated the natural erosion by denuding the countryside of its shade trees. Now the policy was being reversed. China was once 22 percent forest—a figure that had been more or less constant throughout the country's history. But beginning in the 1950s, the trees were cut away and new fields constructed. By the year 2000, the percentage of the countryside covered by trees had been reduced to a paltry six. That deforestation was a prime cause of southern flooding and of northern desertification.

Desertification in China, as it is elsewhere, is subject to the self-reinforcing aspects of feedback loops—cutting down trees elevates the local microclimate temperature, which calls for more water to irrigate thirstier crops, which depletes the water tables, which in turn elevates the temperatures further. The whole process is plain in the dusty landscape north of Yulin, in Shaanxi Province, where I spent a morning talking to a professor of forestry at the local community college, Dang Jiang Qi. We talked on a viewing platform hastily constructed for visiting bigwig Jiang Zemin, the now practically retired Chinese premier. The view is instructive. To the north, the reclaimed forest trails off into sand; a few kilometers beyond that the dunes begin. The Great Wall once stood proudly nearby; it has now crumbled into sand and been overrun by dunes, so that only a few vestigial towers remain. On the other three sides the forest stretches to the horizon, neat rows of jack pines mostly, though there were test parcels of half a dozen conifer species. It looks like a success, and indeed it is—several thousand hectares of land have been reclaimed from the desert.

But it isn't nearly enough, as Mr. Dang acknowledged. "When I was a boy," he said, "this was all verdant land, green as far as you could see. Now it is sand, and the sand is growing. We push it back here and there, but we need an effort such as it took to build the Wall itself to really succeed." The work was ongoing, and indeed our filming earlier that day had several times been interrupted by a low-flying military aircraft seconded to seed-laying duties, the plane crisscrossing the area just north of the Great Wall's ruins, putting down a dusty cloud of grass seed. And on every terraced hillside all through the northern province seedlings had been planted. The intention, an official in Xi'an had said, was to double the amount of forest within a decade, from 6 percent to 12.

Outside the northern city of Yulin, however, they were growing rice in the riverbed. To do so, they had imported hundreds of tons of impermeable clay and dumped it into the riverbed so that the water in the paddies wouldn't just seep away. The crops were moderate, but everyone acknowledged they came at a steep price. The river's flow had diminished to a trickle. What had not diminished, however, was the amount of raw sewage pouring into it, or the amounts of industrial and agricultural waste chemicals.

It was not surprising, therefore, that alarming reports occurred throughout 2002 of increasing numbers of red tide algae blooms off China's coasts. Most of the Chinese red tides consisted of two toxic organisms, *Alexandrium* sp. and *Prorocentrium dentatum*, both products of farm and household waste. The State Oceanographic Bureau, charged with monitoring the health of China's seas, is in the process of setting up monitoring stations along the coast in half a dozen provinces. Wu Jingyou, a bureau official, said that their function in 2002 would be to help fishermen cope with these toxic blooms, not to deal with the blooms themselves, which are produced by factors outside local bureaucratic control. In 2001, he said, shaking his head, there had been a record 77 severe red tides, covering a total of more than 15,000 square kilometers. The East China Sea is one of the most polluted marine environments on the planet. The State Environmental Protection Administration Annual Report 2002 reported 27 red tides that year off the coasts of Zhejiang Province alone. Some of them were one meter thick.

Now that China has turned its ponderous bureaucratic attention to the problem, successes have been scored. One of the most dramatic occurred in Chengdu, the ancient capital of Sichuan Province, on the upper reaches of the Yangtze. The city was built at the junction of the Fu and Nan Rivers, themselves part of one of the Yangtze's major tributaries, the Minjiang. As recently as 1995, both rivers were grotesquely polluted; millions of liters of raw sewage poured into both of them each day through open runnels winding through the shantytowns lining their banks. Each had narrowed to a small channel; millions of tons of poisonous silt backed up the water into noxious ponds. The local government began dredging the river in 1993, widening and deepening the channels from 80 to 120 meters. Shantytowns were razed and 100,000 inhabitants relocated and rehoused. Upstream treatment plants intercepted household waste. The transformation was startling, and the city has subsequently won United Nations accolades for its achievement.

With water scarcity reaching the critical stage in sprawling cities like Beijing and Tianjin, the Chinese have dusted off one of Mao Tse-tung's more grandiose schemes, the South to North Project, which envisaged building three gigantic systems to transport water from the water-rich Yangtze to the arid north. As updated by the Politburo's water planners, the project would involve a triple pipe, canal, and aqueduct network with a combined length of almost 3,500 kilometers. If ever completed, the scheme would dwarf not only California's massive water-redistribution system, but also the aptly named Great Man-Made River in the northern Sahara, hitherto, at 32 billion dollars (U.S), the planet's most costly civil engineering project. The official cost estimate of the South to North Project is 58 billion, about twice the price of the Three Gorges Dam, China's most recent and most controversial megaproject, now nearing completion. Almost half a million people would have to be forcibly relocated. Completion of this massive reengineering of China's hydrological resources—in essence, a reengineering of the whole country—would take decades.

Brian Halweil is skeptical. "The three canals combined would, at best, be able to deliver about 60 million cubic meters of water to the north. The water the project can deliver is nowhere near the volume of deficit they are running. It's only about 5 percent of the deficit." The three routes of the diversion scheme each has its own particular challenge. Each would dwarf the Colorado to California water diversions scheme, which is a few hundred miles long and has to traverse only one mountain range.

The western route is the most speculative and uncertain. It would extract water from the upper reaches of the Yangtze and transport it into the Yellow River Basin. Even ignoring the fact that the 1,200-kilometer pipe and canal will take water from Tibetan regions, with all the political controversies that would entail, it will have to carve channels through several rugged mountain passes of 3,000 meters or more and traverse the most arid part of China, with consequent high evaporation rates. The estimated cost of this branch alone is 36 billion dollars.

The central route calls for diverting water north from the Han River, a tributary of the Yangtze, by constructing a new canal to Beijing. To make this canal flow in the right direction, the engineers will have to raise the Danjiangkou Dam and its reservoir about 30 meters, thereby forcing the relocation of more than a quarter of a million villagers in Hubei and Henan. Since even the elevated dam wouldn't hold nearly enough water for the planned diversion as well as for meeting local needs, yet another new canal would have to be built to bring water from the newly built Three Gorges Dam, thereby reducing that project's electricity-generating capacity by more than 5 percent. This canal, too, would have to be punched through several high mountains.

The diversion that will follow the east coast is technically the simplest. For much of its length it would follow the same route carved out by the Grand Canal, another wonder of imperial China, a waterway that once carried silk and rice from the south to the capital. Even this route will require some dozen pumping stations to lift the water from the Yangtze mouth to the plains of Beijing. The real problem, though, will be the quality of the water that reaches the north. Those sections of the Grand Canal still in use are lined with thousands of houseboats, whose inhabitants rely on the canal for waste disposal. In addition, hundreds of villages and towns along the way pour their effluents, untreated, into the canal itself; as a direct consequence, it is hazardous to use the canal's water even for washing. The new canal will also cross some of the country's most polluted river basins.

Plans to remedy all these problems have been announced, though to people on the ground they have so far been invisible. And even given the country's new fretfulness over pollution, some of the remedies, in the phrase of the *New York Times*'s Erik Eckholm, "stretch credibility." The canal is lined with thousands of factories pouring tons of pollutants into the water. Most of these are owned by local authorities that have ignored Beijing's injunctions in the past, as Eckholm points out. Also, sewage-treatment plants would have to be constructed in each of the 119 counties along the route, a daunting task in itself.

Beijing wants all this to be done in time for the 2008 Olympics. Nobody believes this will happen, at least not to any more than shoddy standards. If it does, China will deserve an Olympic gold medal for the new sport of engineering.

SCARCITY

WATER STRESS

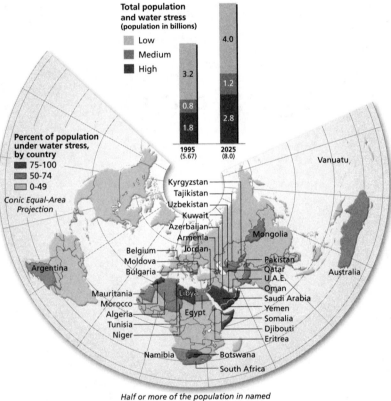

Total population and water stress
(population in billions)

- Low
- Medium
- High

Percent of population under water stress, by country
- 75-100
- 50-74
- 0-49

Conic Equal-Area Projection

	1995 (5.67)	2025 (8.0)
	3.2	4.0
	0.8	1.2
	1.8	2.8

Vanuatu

Kyrgyzstan
Tajikistan
Uzbekistan
Kuwait
Azerbaijan
Armenia
Jordan
Belgium
Moldova
Bulgaria
Argentina
Mongolia
Pakistan
Qatar
U.A.E.
Oman
Australia
Mauritania
Morocco
Algeria
Tunisia
Niger
Libya
Egypt
Saudi Arabia
Yemen
Somalia
Djibouti
Eritrea
Namibia
Botswana
South Africa

Half or more of the population in named countries experience water stress.

The paradox of any serious discussion about water is how this watery planet has increasingly become one in which there is water scarcity. Some suggest that it's not a question of scarcity but one of allocation, supply, and management. Others say it's our collective will in solving water problems that is lacking rather than the water itself. Some believe that water scarcity has been driven by greed. And many experts agree that the world is not short of water, but only short of usable water.

There does at least seem to be consensus on the sheer magnitude of freshwater problems. But huge gaps exist in our understanding and our ability to respond, not just to issues of scarcity but to their complex relationship to poverty, population, pollution, and international boundaries.

Growing evidence shows that population growth, severely inadequate water supply, and poverty are inextricably linked. A country is identified as having a serious water problem when the amount of available water drops below 1,000 cubic meters per person per year. This affects the general health and economic development of a country. When the amount drops below 500 cubic meters, survival is compromised. Many of the world's poorest live in areas of drought and high temperatures. Forty of the fifty countries generally recognized as short of water are located in the Middle East and in north and sub-Saharan Africa. In fact, nine out of the fourteen Middle Eastern nations already face water scarcity. The global trend is disturbing; many experts agree that since 1970 the water supply has declined by 33 percent. At the moment, 60 percent of the world's people are living in Asia, which has only 36 percent of the world's renewable fresh water. By 2015 an estimated 3 billion people will live in countries facing water shortages. Even at present, the World Health Organization believes that more than 1 billion people lack access to clean drinking water and nearly 2.5 billion lack improved sanitation services.

It's clear that we are currently taking more than we are replenishing. Human intervention into the hydrological cycle—the natural ecological process by which water is replaced—appears to be tipping the balance toward a serious deficit. Forest floors that remain covered in leaves and humus retain water and regenerate water tables, but extensive logging and monoculture agriculture allow that water to run off. The Cherapunji region in northeast India receives 11 meters of rainfall a year but, with its forests gone, it now has a drinking problem. Serious denuding of mountain slopes in the Himalaya has resulted in massive slope collapses and subsequent downstream flooding. Eucalyptus monoculture in South Africa resulted in dried-up streams and depleted groundwater stores; in this case, replanting with a variety of species was followed by a 120 percent increase in the streams' capacity.

The emerging facts on water scarcity are disturbing and widespread. In merely three years northern China's water tables plummeted four meters. Major rivers no longer reach the sea for months on end. The Yellow River failed to reach the sea for 226 days in 1997. The Colorado River frequently runs dry before reaching the ocean, mostly because of overallocation of water to users in the upper basins. The level of the Dead Sea has plummeted more than 10 meters this century; the Jordan River has been reduced to little more than a trickle, thanks to substantial redistribution from Jordan to Israel. Lake Chad is shrinking at a rate of nearly 100 meters a year.

Scarcity of usable water has been seriously aggravated by pollution. Steady global economic growth, where not accompanied by appropriate pollution regulation and enforcement, has devastated water supplies. From small mountain village streams in the Himalaya to the supercanals of southern China, unrestricted effluents and chemical and industrial waste are befouling the water supply. Red tides, up to a meter thick with toxic organisms, clog the East China Sea. The water quality of Siberia's Lake Baykal, the largest freshwater lake in the world, is deteriorating steadily as effluents from unregulated factories pour into it. Within our lifetimes, the productivity of the Great Lakes in North America has declined dramatically through eutrophication, the excess algal growth stimulated by phosphates. Their shores are frequently posted with signs reading "Unfit for swimming." Preventable water-related diseases still kill enormous numbers— an estimated 10,000 to 20,000 children worldwide—each day.

A direct link exists between water and food, and the growing number of hungry mouths is accelerating the shortages of water. About 70 percent of freshwater use is for agriculture, and close to 10 percent of those water sources are almost exhausted. Historically, the exact variety of food production established in certain areas was dependent upon the amount of readily available water: Wet regions of Asia produced rice, arid regions of the prairies produced wheat and other cereal grains, deserts relied on pastoral cultivation. The green revolution and industrial agriculture have changed all that. The green revolution emphasized high-yield seeds and water-guzzling crops. Starvation of millions of people was prevented, but the ecological cost has not been completely acknowledged.

Industrial agriculture has pushed food production to seemingly unsustainable levels. Irrigation projects have led to water-intensive farming, but the results have included waterlogging and salination of huge areas of land, eventually leading to decreased productivity and finally to desertification.

One of the most spectacular examples of unsustainable agriculture is the Aral Sea region, fourth largest freshwater body, now two-thirds gone. With salinity levels soaring and the water level dropping like a stone, it has even lost the benefit of its feeder rivers, whose volumes are being diverted to huge irrigation canals many miles away. Twenty-four species of fish formerly found in the Aral's waters are now extinct. Salinity levels in the Pecos River, the Rio Grande, the Colorado, and other southwestern U.S. rivers are also alarming.

The future of irrigated agriculture is becoming increasingly vulnerable. Crops that rely heavily on irrigation are most often found in areas where groundwater is being overpumped and rivers are running dry. Severe examples exist in the Punjab area of India, China's northern plains, Iran, and the Indus Basin in Pakistan. The groundwater issue is particularly problematic because it is a somewhat invisible problem. Aquifer water levels are also falling at an alarming rate, such as the Ogallala Aquifer in Texas, which produces up to eight million acre-feet of water each year. Experts are convinced such water extraction is not sustainable, and yet mechanized water-withdrawal systems have been promoted and subsidized around the world, including in traditional pastoral areas of Africa. Once the wells are in place, settlement becomes concentrated, grazing pressure increases in specific areas—and water tables drop.

Water quality is also in decline, particularly in the major cities of the developing world, which are bursting at their seams. Yet even in Canada, Torontonions prefer bottled water to tap water, and with good reason. According to aquatic ecologist Jack

Vallentyne, a glass of tap water in Toronto includes a toxic mix of fluorocarbons, PCBs, pesticides, and tetrachloride.

The sheer number of thirsty people is a growing issue. Although the rate of population growth has slowed dramatically, we will still add two billion more to the global population by the mid 21st century. Even more troubling, our rate of water consumption is more than twice that of the rate of population growth. This dramatic change is also unsustainable.

The upstream-downstream link has not been adequately acknowledged or understood. Almost all major rivers have their sources in mountains, and more than half of humanity relies on water from these rivers for domestic use, irrigation, industry, and the generation of hydroelectric power. These downward-flowing waters are also essential to the health of ecosystems, providing nutrients for aquatic life and diluting pollutants generated mostly in lowland areas. In the years to come, those "water towers" will become even more critical as urbanization and the intensification of agriculture threaten to deplete and contaminate existing groundwater sources. Although nearly 50 percent of the global population currently lives in urban regions, that number is expected to rise to 60 percent in the next 30 years, placing enormous strain on the lowland water supply, most of which comes from the mountains. Given a need to increase food production by at least 50 percent over the next three decades, farming will contribute a substantial additional strain.

How will we address the worldwide water crisis? Fortunately, it appears more and more to be one caused by the ways we mismanage water rather than real scarcity. The essays that follow address specific problems and what we can do about them. Margaret Catley-Carlson focuses on the need to break the vicious cycle linking poverty and water shortage. Lester R. Brown makes a strong case that food production will be seriously jeopardized in the future if water tables keep falling due to overpumping. Hans Schreier looks to the mountains and to mountain people for some creative solutions to downstream water problems. One thing seems clear—we cannot wait too long to protect that most precious of natural resources: water.

WORKING FOR WATER

Margaret Catley-Carlson

Asmall-town Kenyan woman keeps her daughter out of school in order to walk miles to get the family's water for the day. In Pakistan, a group of schoolchildren write and perform a play that pokes fun at the bejeweled begums who use their influence and a little cash to divert city water trucks toward their swimming pools or to wash their driveways. In northern Syria a farmer laments that he will have to move everything—the sheep, goats, both wives, all the children, and the new drip-irrigation equipment—if the rainfall continues to decline.

In terms of planetary supply, the simplest way to understand the scarcity of water is this: If all the water in the world were compared to a one-liter bottle, there is but a single drop of fresh water to grow crops with, drink, wash, and power industries, once salt water and water in ice caps have been subtracted. And this small amount is not distributed evenly in time or space. The Amazon alone contains 10 percent of global freshwater supply—which doesn't help the Middle East. In parts of India, more than 90 percent of the annual rain falls in a few days—it doesn't help the rest of the year.

The world's demand for water is doubling every 20 years. With populations increasing and less water left in the streams or the aquifers, that amount of available water per person is declining, often rapidly. The danger signs are manifold. Water tables are declining; many important rivers, such as the Yellow and the Colorado, no longer reach the sea for months on end. More than 1.1 billion people do not have consistent access to fresh water, and more than twice that number lack access to sanitation. Close to 10 percent of water sources being used primarily by agriculture are almost exhausted. Deltas and wetlands are disappearing. In one stark case, 90 percent of California's wetlands have already disappeared. The levels of aquifers, the essential underground layers of porous rock or sand containing water, are falling in many places, including northern China and the Ogallala Aquifer in Texas. And water quality everywhere is in decline, nowhere more than in the burgeoning cities of the developing world, where most of the world's population will live by the end of the current decade.

At no time in history has there been such a magnitude of fresh-water problems. There is even increasing agreement on the instruments and directions of much-needed remedial policies. Although all aspects are interrelated, there are discrete issues of concern: water for people, water for food, water for the environment, and the investment and management tools needed to overcome these problems.

Although the *rate* of population growth has slowed dramatically, the rapid growth of the last few generations means that *actual* population growth will continue at quite a rapid rate, resulting in two billion people more by the midpoint of the next century. Experts see a leveling off at a range of 7.5 billion to a UN-predicted 9.3 billion around 2070. But while world population has trebled, water use has increased more than sixfold.

Urbanization will continue at an even faster pace than overall population growth. The growing cities will need food—and water. However, municipal water infrastructures cost money to build and maintain. Within decades, most poverty will be urban poverty. If half of the population of a city is living below the poverty line, the tax base and the capacity to provide services are both negatively affected. A dramatic manifestation of that poverty will be water shortage in cities, and what water that is available will be of increasingly poor quality.

Water is closely connected to income and to nourishment. Agriculture uses a little more than 70 percent of water abstractions in the developing nations. Roughly 800 million people live in a state of severe malnourishment, particularly in India and parts of Africa. This occurs in a world where total food production is close to 3,000 calories per person per day. At one time a general increase in food availability was thought to be the primary solution to malnourish-ment—and it helps—but increasing the income of poor people is even more essential. The largest percentage of the poor is as yet rural. People living in rural areas must be able to grow food and sell it.

Climate change will in all likelihood intensify all of these problems because the poorest people—and it is being poor that is the fundamental precondition for ill health and malnutri-tion—live in many of the areas likely to feel the impacts: more droughts and higher temperatures. Of the nearly 50 countries that are now short of water, or will be by 2025, 40 are in the Middle East and north or sub-Saharan Africa.

Malnourished people who live on less than one dollar (U.S.) a day are often found in areas lacking water. In most com-munities in the world women are the water gatherers and food providers. Because they spend more and more time traveling great distances to find water for daily basic use, little time is left over for growing food. To add to the problem, in most of these very poor areas, population growth continues to be high.

Because they have to fetch water, or because they have been pulled from school at puberty because of the lack of separate toi-lets, or because their families don't believe in the value of education, girls in these areas too often do not attend school. This causes a critical problem, as uneducated girls marry earlier and have more children than those with even a few years of education. World Bank research has noted that primary education for girls has resulted in more community improvement than any other factor in the areas of food production, family nutrition, water management, community-level income, and family health.

In the foothills of the Aberdares in Kenya, I met a former teacher at the village school who had quit because both she and her students had to venture farther each day to fetch water. We were together at the opening of a village water pipe where sweat equity had dug trenches and CIDA (Canadian International Development Agency) had supplied pipes to bring water to the village from the mountains. Happily, she said she and her girls were going back to school.

Scarcity is not the sole issue; poor quality water is also a threat. Waterborne diseases (cholera, typhoid, diarrhea), diseases caused by lack of bathing water (scabies, trachoma), diseases of parasites in contaminated water (schistosomiasis, helminthiasis), and water-related diseases, from water-living or water-breeding insects (dengue, river blindness, malaria)—all of these create a death toll that mounts to five million a year. This means every minute of the day ten persons die unnecessary deaths. According to the UN World Water Development Report, the majority are children under five.

The world is trying to respond to these growing crises. At the United Nations in 2000, the world's governments pledged to reduce by half, by 2015, the proportion of people that are malnourished and that do not have access to safe water. The Johannesburg Earth Summit added a similar target for sanitation. These goals sound wonderful, but in fact imply incredibly ambitious, if not impossible, enterprises. In the 4,400 days remaining till 2015, every day about 274,000 additional people would have to gain access to clean water and over 342,000 to sanitation for these goals to be met. This is simply not going to happen given the current low priority accorded to water in national budgets. And even if that 2015 target were met, close to 700 million would still be left out. This means that water-related deaths totaling tens of millions will continue in the decades ahead.

A major challenge is financing. The World Water Commission reported to the 2000 Hague Ministerial Conference that while 70 billion dollars are currently being spent each year on water management, 170 billion dollars are needed to address the problem of the 1.1 billion people without water access, the 2.4 billion without sewage facilities, and the treatment of water and sewage from cities—the systemic costs of sewage and water cleanup need to be considered part of the water management budget.

How is the future of water to be funded? The World Bank estimates that current total investment in water and sanitation is around 30 billion dollars (U.S.) per year, with a remaining 70 billion in water investment going to hydropower developments and irrigation. Currently, water supply and sanitation services are largely funded by the public sector, which is under increasing pressure.

It is clear that new and innovative financing mechanisms are desperately needed. Even in wealthy nations such as Canada and the United States, municipal water infrastructure needs will cost trillions of dollars over the next decade. The infrastructure needs of the developing world will amount to equally staggering amounts in the next decades, and public institutions will not be able to produce the needed funding.

But there is hope. Community energy and dedication are two of the great underused resources that can be mobilized to meet water supply and sanitation needs. A large part of the funding gap could be filled for relatively small amounts of money, if the world were serious about community collaboration.

For example, Sheila Patel has mobilized women in cities in India to construct and manage latrines—both to clean up their own communities and later to earn revenue by extending their services to other communities. In order to support this type of initiative, governments must seek them out, offer financing, and get behind these efforts.

The private sector also has a role. It can bring expertise in both technology and management, and can organize financing for water infrastructures and services. However, private sector involvement in water-service delivery is controversial. Experience has taught that a number of preconditions are needed for success. Elected representatives and civil society must be able to conduct a constructive debate on the issues of the private sector contract: service levels, price setting, and service extensions. Some form of transparent monitoring is needed with reliable information made publicly available so that decisions can be well informed. Affordable access to the improvements must be safeguarded as well.

Regardless of the ideological viewpoint on who should pay, it is clear that the supply and use of water entails expenditures. The question of how these costs are going to be addressed and how payments will apply at the household, city, metropolitan area, and national levels must be publicly debated. The plans among water users may be different for drinking water, wastewater, or irrigation.

Essentially, water management must change. Water systems will run better if people pay in their capacity as water users rather than as taxpayers, although some may well require subsidies to meet their water, sanitation, and livelihood needs.

There is increasing agreement on the instruments and needed directions of other remedial policies and practices. Integrated water resource management is essential. Separate and uncoordinated activity by irrigation, water and sanitation, hydro and flood authorities is unlikely to lead to unified water policy with precious water resources consciously allocated to promote public good.

There is no single template for a well-managed system, but it will probably include the creation and enforcement of appropriate policies, laws, and regulatory frameworks. There will be increased public participation processes at all levels (national, basin or subbasin, municipal, local community) and somewhat more power-sharing in the consultative and decision-making processes. Water arrangements should be transparent arrangements, especially regarding water-allocation decision-making between and within sectors. Improved and equitable service delivery by public and private operators needs to be backstopped by publicly available service standards and financial accounts. The Global Water Partnership is an example of an organization dedicated to the task of promoting this kind of change to move the world toward sustainable water management.

The Murray Darling River Basin covers about one-third of Australia. The basin accounts for over 75 percent of Australia's agricultural exports and a high percentage of Australia's overall population and productivity. For the past century, the rivers in this basin have been diverted, exploited, and harnessed for human use. As a consequence, there have been increasing levels of soil salinity, water salinity, and despoiling of important national sites such as the Snowy River. Two decades ago, several Australian states began to address the problem through a consultative process that has become a model. Assembling the consultative process—examining the role of governments, building public awareness, and including agricultural agencies, farmers, and regulators—has been slow and complex, but it is working. And now this model is being used in Vietnam and in the Mekong Commission.

Rivers and aquifers don't follow political borders. So although national governments are crucial to improved water management, some governance arrangements must also apply to a whole river, even when it crosses several borders. All over the world now dozens of river basin associations are being organized, with the European Union leading the way. Their Framework Directive insists on wastewater treatment and on public debate around water management issues. They are moving toward water basin management.

One river basin system can learn much by studying the management regimes of other water basins. Brazil has been pioneering a new approach against pollution: The government "buys" clean water returned to rivers. In India, the Friends of the Purna River are working together to find solutions to salinity that poses threats to both drinking water and the farmlands. Such successes should be implemented and built upon.

In Canada, the Fraser River Basin group provides an inspiring and much emulated example. This group approaches the sustainability and future economic health of the river from an integrated approach that includes economic, social, and environmental considerations. Home to 2.6 million people, the Fraser River Basin extends from the river's headwaters in the Canadian Rockies to its delta in Richmond, British Columbia. The California-size basin covers over one-quarter of the province, supports diverse ecosystems, and accounts for 80 percent of British Columbia's economic activity.

Formed just over five years ago, the nonprofit, nonpartisan Fraser Basin Council brings a broad range of stakeholders together: small and large businesses, environmental stewards, agriculturists and ranchers, tourism promoters, local governments, flood-hazard managers, and community economic developers. The council's mandate is focused on the future well-being of the river and its communities. All levels of government are represented as well as First Nations, the private sector, environmental organizations, and community groups. The result is an integrated and inclusive approach that proves it is possible to oppose bad planning and execution of systems rather than the systems. Dams and irrigation are not in themselves a problem; what is problematic is the thoughtless use of water for any purpose. Transparency and monitoring for all water-delivery systems, such as the Fraser Basin Council exhibits, can alleviate the vilifying of ideas and focus on the processes of carrying out these ideas.

Finally, we need to take care of water itself. Constant economic growth, where not accompanied by appropriate pollution regulations and enforcement, has devastated water supplies. Nature can no longer restore itself—the disappearance of wetlands, habitats, and species attests to this fact.

In our world, we take water, store it, pipe it, measure and calibrate it, purify it, deliver it, and then flush 40 percent of it down the drain. This is not a logical way to manage water. We must work harder to allocate water between users and ecosystems in an effort to achieve sustainable development and reduce poverty. We have to look to the success stories that exist and learn from them. Whether it's a water basin management group, forward-thinking government legislation, or a group of women in India, we have an opportunity to learn how to use water wisely.

THE EFFECT OF EMERGING WATER

SHORTAGES ON THE WORLD'S FOOD

Lester R. Brown

n August 2001, a little-noticed study released in Beijing brought attention unexpectedly to what was already a grim picture of China's water situation. It showed that the water table under the North China Plain, which produces over half of China's wheat and a third of its corn, was falling faster than thought. Overpumping had largely depleted the shallow aquifer, reducing the amount of water that can be pumped from it to the amount of recharge from precipitation. That was forcing well drillers to draw from the region's deep aquifer, one that is not replenishable.

Under Heibei Province in the heart of the North China Plain, the average level of the deep aquifer had dropped 2.9 meters (nearly 10 feet) in 2000 alone. Around some cities in the province, it fell by 6 meters, said the study, conducted by the Geological Environmental Monitoring Institute in Beijing. A separate report by the World Bank said deep wells drilled around Beijing "now have to reach 1,000 meters to tap fresh water, adding dramatically to the cost of supply." It forecast "catastrophic consequences for future generations" unless water use and supply could quickly be brought back into balance.

What might those consequences be? Pumping from such depths translates into exorbitant costs and reduced profit margins, often forcing farmers back to dryland farming. Already, China's grain harvest has begun to diminish, and falling water tables appear to be an important reason, along with reduced government grain-support prices and the loss of farm labor in provinces that are rapidly industrializing. The wheat crop, grown mostly in the more arid northern part of China, is particularly vulnerable to water shortages. After peaking at 123 million tons in 1997, the harvest has fallen in four of the last five years, to an estimated 87 million tons in 2003. Overall, China's grain harvest has dropped by 13 percent or 50 million tons—an amount equivalent to Canada's total grain production.

The U.S. Embassy in Beijing also reports that the recent decline in rice production is partly the result of water shortages. After peaking at 140 million tons in 1997, the harvest has dropped in each of the five years since then, falling to 121 million tons in 2002. These precipitous harvest declines for the world's leading producer of both wheat and rice do not auger well for the future.

Unfortunately, China is not alone. Scores of countries are overpumping aquifers as they struggle to satisfy their growing water needs, and falling water tables are starting to affect harvests in many of them. Aquifers are being extensively overpumped in the two other leading grain-producing countries—India and the United States—which, along with China, collectively account for half of the world grain harvest. Their populations, combined with those of other countries, including Pakistan, Mexico, and Iran, where overpumping will measurably reduce the food supply when aquifers are depleted, exceed three billion people. Half of the world's people live in countries where aquifer depletion threatens to reduce future food supplies.

If we are facing a future of water scarcity, then we are also facing a future of food scarcity. In effect, many countries have created a food bubble economy, one where food production is artificially inflated by the unsustainable use of water. Overpumping and the resultant depletion of aquifers will reduce the water available for irrigation in many societies, including those in China and India—the two countries that together contain nearly 40 percent of the world's people.

At what point does water scarcity translate into food scarcity? In which countries will the loss of irrigation water because of aquifer depletion translate into an absolute decline in grain production? David Seckler and his colleagues at the International Water Management Institute offer a bleak assessment. "Many of the most populous countries of the world—China, India, Pakistan, Mexico, and nearly all the countries of the Middle East and North Africa—have literally been having a free ride over the past two or three decades by depleting their groundwater resources. The penalty of mismanagement of this valuable resource is now coming due and it is no exaggeration to say that the results could be catastrophic for these countries, and given their importance, for the world as a whole."

The link between water supplies and food supplies is a strong one. Seventy percent of all the water diverted from rivers or pumped from underground worldwide is used for irrigation. Twenty percent is used by industry and 10 percent for residential purposes. But in the rivalry over water, farmers are increasingly losing out to cities and industry, sometimes in negotiations, sometimes by fiat. There are ways for farmers to use water more efficiently, but when overall demand is greater than the supply, it is most often farmers who are under pressure.

For now, the water deficit is largely invisible. Because it typically takes the form of aquifer overpumping and falling water tables, it cannot be seen. Nor, unlike burning forests or invading sand dunes, can falling water tables be readily photographed. They are often discovered only when wells go dry.

Water scarcity was once a local issue, but it has begun to cross international boundaries via the international grain trade. Countries that are pressing against the limits of their water supply typically satisfy the growing needs of cities and industry by diverting irrigation water from agriculture, then importing grain to offset the loss of productive capacity. Because of the 1,000:1 production ratio between water and grain, importing grain is the most efficient way to import water. As water shortages intensify, so too will the competition for grain in international markets.

Irrigation water has played a crucial role in the tripling of the world grain harvest from 1950 to 2000. So it should come as no surprise that a loss of irrigation water could contribute to an actual decline in production. After two or three decades of overpumping and falling water tables, the list of depleted aquifers is growing fast.

Most of the aquifers in India and the shallow aquifer under the North China Plain are replenishable. If a replenishable aquifer is being overpumped at, say, double the rate of recharge, then aquifer depletion will cut the amount of water pumped in half.

If an aquifer happens to be a fossil aquifer, or nonreplenishable, such as the vast Ogallala Aquifer under the Great Plains of the United States, the deep aquifer under the North China Plain, or the aquifer under Saudi Arabia, then depletion brings pumping to an end. Farmers who lose their irrigation water supply entirely usually have the option of returning to lower-yield dryland farming, except in desert situations, such as parts of the southwestern United States or in some countries in the Middle East. Here, the loss of irrigation water means the end of agriculture.

Once the growing demand for water rises above the sustainable yield of an aquifer, the gap between the two widens further each year. The first year after the line is crossed, the water table falls very little, with the drop often being scarcely perceptible. Each year thereafter, however, the annual drop in the water table is larger than the year before.

In addition to declining exponentially, water tables are also falling at the same time in scores of countries. The overpumping of aquifers, occurring in so many places at the same time, means that aquifer depletion and the resulting harvest cutbacks will also come at roughly the same time. And the accelerating depletion of aquifers means depletion may come sooner than expected. The diesel-driven or electrically driven pumps that make over-pumping possible have become available throughout the entire world at essentially the same time. The simultaneous cutbacks in grain harvests will be occurring at a time when the world's population is growing by more than 70 million per year. This could create a potentially disastrous cut in the food supply.

Food shortage crises are impending in a number of countries. In India, where roughly half of the irrigated land is watered with surface water and roughly half with underground water, David Seckler and colleagues have estimated that the pumping of groundwater may be taking place at a rate double that which could be naturally recharged. Overpumping is taking place in several states, including the Punjab (India's breadbasket), Haryana, Gujarat, Rajasthan, Andhra Pradesh, and Tamil Nadu. Beneath the Punjab and Haryana, water tables are falling by up to one meter per year. Data for monitored wells in Gujarat indicate that the water table has fallen from a depth of 15 meters to 400 meters over the past three decades. At this point, the harvest of wheat and rice, India's principal food grains, is still increasing. Exactly when the loss of irrigation water will override technological progress and start shrinking the harvest, as it is already doing in China, is not clear, but it could occur within the next few years.

The water shortages in Iran, a country of 66 million people, are quickly becoming acute. Under the small, but agriculturally rich, Chenaran Plain in northeastern Iran, the water table was falling by 2.8 meters a year in the late 1990s. But in 2001, the cumulative effect of a three-year drought and the new wells being drilled both for irrigation and to supply the nearby city of Mashad dropped the aquifer by an extraordinary eight meters. Villages in eastern Iran are being abandoned as wells go dry, generating a flow of water refugees.

Saudi Arabia, a country of 23 million people, has tried to develop an extensive irrigated agriculture based largely on deep fossil aquifers. But it is as water poor as it is oil rich. After several years of supporting the price of wheat at five times the world market level to encourage farmers to develop an irrigated culture based on these deep aquifers, the government has been forced to face fiscal reality and cut back on the program. Even so, available data indicate the fossil aquifer is being depleted and could run dry within the next decade. At this point, irrigated agriculture will largely disappear, limited to the small area that can be irrigated with water from the shallow aquifers that are replenished by the kingdom's sparse rainfall.

Yemen, a country of 19 million, is fast becoming a hydrological basket case. The water table under most of the country is falling by roughly two meters a year. In the Sana'a basin in western Yemen, the estimated annual water extraction exceeds the annual recharge by a factor of five, causing the water table to drop by six meters per year. The World Bank projects that the Sana'a Basin, home to two million people, will be pumped dry by the end of this decade. The Yemeni government has drilled test wells in the basin that are two kilometers (1.2 miles) deep, but has failed to find water. With its population growing by 3.5 percent a year, Yemen must soon decide whether to bring water to Sana'a, possibly by pipeline from coastal desalting plants, or to relocate the capital. Either alternative will be costly and potentially traumatic.

Israel, despite its pioneering work in raising irrigation water productivity, is depleting its two principal aquifers, one of which it shares with the Palestinians. Conflicts between Israelis and Palestinians over the allocation of water in the mountain aquifer are ongoing. The severity of shortages in Israel, which imports over 90 percent of its grain, had led to the phasing out of irrigated wheat production.

In Mexico, too, the demand for water is outstripping supply. In the agricultural state of Guanajuato, for example, the water table is falling by two meters or more a year. At the national level—in a country of 104 million, with the population projected to reach 150 million by 2050—more than half of the water extracted from underground is coming from aquifers that are being overpumped.

Although reliable projections about the future transfer of irrigation water to residential and industrial uses do not yet exist for many countries, World Bank calculations for South Korea, a relatively well-watered country, give some sense of what might lie ahead. The Bank's analysts calculated that if the Korean economy grows 5.5 percent annually until 2025, growth in water withdrawals for residential and industrial use would reduce the supply available for agriculture from 13 billion tons at present to 7 billion tons in 2025. Ignoring the potential for reusing industrial or domestic water in agriculture or the potential effect of raising water prices on demand, this would reduce the water available for irrigation by nearly half.

For the countries that are depleting their aquifers, might surface water provide a substitute? Unfortunately, here the situation is generally just as bleak, because rivers are often the first resources to be exhausted. In Egypt, the Nile once carried some 32 billion cubic meters of water into the Mediterranean each year. After the Aswan Dam was built in the 1960s, and as irrigation and other demands on the river increased, it declined to less than two billion cubic meters. A similar situation exists with the Tigris and Euphrates Rivers, which originate in Turkey and flow into Syria and Iraq en route to the Persian Gulf. This river system, the site of Sumer and other early civilizations, is being used at full capacity.

The loss of river flow can affect the health of estuaries and inland lakes and seas. The Helmand River, which originates in the mountains of eastern Afghanistan, flows westward across the country and into Iran, where it empties into Lake Hamoun. When the Taliban built a new dam on the Helmand during the late 1990s, in violation of a water-sharing agreement between the two countries, they effectively removed all the remaining water. As a result, the river no longer flows into Iran. Lake Hamoun, now a dry lake bed, once covered 4,000 square kilometers. The abandoned fishing villages on its shores are being covered by sand dunes arising from the lake bed itself.

A similar situation exists with the Aral Sea. The Amu Darya, which along with the Syr Darya is one of the two rivers feeding the Aral Sea, is drained dry by Uzbek and Turkmen cotton farmers upstream. As a result, the Aral Sea has shrunk about 58 percent in size and has lost 83 percent of its volume of water. The loss of freshwater recharge and the loss of volume have led to a dramatic rise in salt levels and the demise of the once abundant fisheries. In addition to sandstorms, the region now suffers from salt storms arising from the exposed seabed.

In China, a World Bank study undertaken several years ago indicated that China was overpumping three river basins in the north—the Hai, which flows through Beijing and Tianjin; the Yellow; and the Huai, the next river south of the Yellow—by 37 billion tons per year. Given what is taking place in these basins, one could conservatively assume that the overpumping in the northern half of China easily exceeds 40 billion tons of water per year.

The Yellow River, the cradle of Chinese civilization, flows 4,000 kilometers through seven provinces before it reaches the Yellow Sea, but it has been under mounting pressure for several decades. It first ran dry in 1972, failing to reach the sea. Since 1985 it has failed to reach the sea for part of almost every year. As China attempts to accelerate the economic development of the upper Yellow River Basin, developing industries upstream get priority in the use of water. As more and more water is used upstream, less reaches farmers downstream. Not only does the Yellow River fail to reach the sea, but sometimes it fails to reach Shandong, the last province that it flows through en route to sea. Farmers in Shandong have traditionally gotten roughly half of their irrigation water from the Yellow River and half from wells. Now they are losing water from both sources as the river flow is reduced and local aquifers are depleted. As a supplier of grain, Shandong is more important to China than Iowa and Kansas together are to the United States, producing a fifth of China's corn and a seventh of its wheat, so that helps to explain why China's grain production has been declining in recent years.

And yet, in China and around the world, cities are continuing to grow, and their water needs can be voracious. Many cities are located in basins where all water is now being used. Cities in these watersheds, such as Cairo and Beijing, can measurably increase their water consumption only by taking water from agriculture. In the United States, San Diego, Los Angeles, Phoenix, Las Vegas, Denver, and El Paso are in a comparable situation. That has produced a boom in the western United States in the sales of water rights, which may be approaching as much as one percent per year of underground water used for irrigation, according to an extrapolation of a study conducted in 11 states by the U.S. Department of Agriculture for 1996 and 1997. If this loss of irrigation water in the 11 states is combined with water-rights sales in other states and water loss from aquifer depletion, the decline in underground irrigation water could be approaching 2 percent a year, or 20 percent per decade.

In the competition for water among farmers, cities, and industry, the short-term economics of water use never favor farmers; more water is required to produce food than any other economic good. The thousand tons of water required to produce a ton of wheat are enough to produce 16 tons of steel, with a value many times greater than that of grain. But the long-term consequence of so many short-term decisions may soon be upon us. The question—in China, India, and other countries as well—is not whether the water-for-food bubble will burst, but when.

MOUNTAIN WISE AND

WATER SMART

Hans Schreier

n a mountain watershed in the Jiri region of Nepal, farmers
have developed an intricate agricultural system comprising
a sequence of over 300 terraces carved out of the mountains
several generations ago. The farmers have converted this
slope into 15,000 small plots. Water is supplied to each plot
through an ingenious irrigation system fed by three small streams.
Although the allocation of water might be traditional, farmers
have embraced part of the green revolution—the increase in
productivity through irrigation, improved strains of seeds, and

fertilizers—to keep up with food demands by a rapidly growing rural population. The indigenous water-management system developed by the farmers is capable of delivering water to each of the 15,000 fields at the beginning of the monsoon season over a two- to three-week period in order to grow rice. In fact, farmers are now growing two and, in some favorable microclimatic conditions, three crops per year.

It is a fascinating landscape, but it masks the effort that goes into maintaining this system. A development project, cosponsored by the International Development Research Centre (IDRC) and the Swiss Agency for Development and Cooperation (SDC), is currently being undertaken in this area. Together with Nepali partners under the leadership of P.B. Shah, work is being done with the farmers during the pre-monsoon season on aspects of soil erosion protection and fertility maintenance. The work that goes into terrace stabilization is enormous. During this period each farmer scrapes a four- to eight-inch layer of soil and rocks from the terrace risers, fills in holes, and stabilizes any weaknesses in the terrace system. Without this effort, terrace failures during the monsoon season would affect the food security of everyone who cultivates crops in the terraces below. Each farmer has to maintain his terraces, for without a coordinated effort, the entire system would collapse.

This singular example is indicative of what is happening around the world in order to provide enough food for people to eat. Agriculture globally uses 70 percent of the Earth's freshwater resources and, with 17 percent of the arable land irrigated, is able to produce 40 percent of all food. Water-use efficiency has not been a concern until recently, but with the introduction of two to three crop rotations a year and the increasing demand for water from outside the watershed, water problems are becoming more acute. How can the system deal with the added pressure when the capacity of the current system is already under stress?

The answer can be found in the mountains. Mountains have an enormous impact on all inhabitants of the world because they are the water towers of humanity; they control, store, and release water. Two-thirds of all fresh water is frozen in glacial ice, and a good portion of glacial ice is in the mountains. Globally, mountains harbor great biodiversity and have unique recreational value, but regulating fresh water is definitely the most important function of mountains.

Learning how mountains regulate the hydrologic cycle and how mountain water resources fit into the emerging global picture is crucial. Unfortunately, the level of research in mountains is inadequate, and understanding of the key hydrologic processes is poor. The seasonal shift from snow to rain cannot be determined accurately by remote means and a weak field observation base. Some 75 percent of all stream flow monitoring stations are located at elevations below 500 meters (1,600 feet), yet most water is stored at higher elevations in snow, ice, and alpine lakes and rivers.

Not only is there a lack of knowledge about stream flow, but understanding of glacial dynamics is also inadequate. The best knowledge of glaciers has been collected in the European Alps, where there is a long history of glacier monitoring. However, this knowledge is of limited value; if all of the Alpine glaciers melted due to global warming, the total contribution to a rise in sea level would be less than 5 percent. The largest continental glaciers are in the Himalaya, where the knowledge base is almost nonexistent. Yet almost one-third of humanity depends on the waters from this mountain region. Tropical glaciers, which are those under the greatest threat, have been studied by only a very few.

Climate change looms heavily over the mountain peaks, and the glaciers are melting far faster than experts predicted. This is welcome news for the many people who live in the parched lowlands of the world's arid zones. Most major rivers originate in mountains, and they provide life support for people who live in the lowlands traversed by the water on its way to the ocean. Climate warming is generating more—and prolonged—runoff from glaciers and, for the next few years, this increased stream flow is giving a false impression of security to the thirsty lowland populations. They desperately need to increase food production, and at the same time satisfy domestic and industrial use for their rapidly growing cities. In the years to come, mountain water towers will become even more critical because, once the glaciers shrink beyond a critical mass, most river runoff will be determined solely by rainfall. The inevitable result is much greater stream flow variability, which in turn will result in more frequent floods and periods of prolonged drought downstream.

Lonnie Thompson, a pioneer in glacial ice-core analysis,[1] has been climbing glaciers for the past 25 years in an effort to extract the historic record of ice accumulation. He received very little support and attention in the early 1970s when he started to collect ice cores in Peru. Since then he has accumulated nearly four miles of ice cores from a wide range of tropical and temperate glaciers. All have been analyzed and safely stored in his ice lab at Ohio State

University. His most challenging work was the coring of Tibetan glaciers at 21,000 to 23,000 feet (6,500 to 7,000 meters). Helicopters could not be used because of the elevation, so the cores were cut into 12-foot sections and carried out in insulated coolers on the backs of yaks. Some of Thompson's most dramatic findings suggest that the Kilimanjaro Glacier will disappear within the next 15 to 20 years.[2] The fate of many glaciers in the Andean and Himalayan regions is also in question. Mountains provide the most sensitive signal on how climate change will shape hydrology in the future.[3] Glaciers store 66 percent of all the fresh water, and scientists can determine the amount of water stored in the glaciers and measure the dynamic fluxes from year to year. It is possible to model changes under different temperature regimes and calculate annual water balances. Glaciers do not respond to individual weather events but respond to long-term shifts in temperature and precipitation. They provide an integrated picture of long-term trends; current findings show continuing losses of glacial mass each year and accelerating rates of losses. Few people have contemplated what a world without mountain glaciers will look like and what the long-term consequences will be.

Fifteen years of development work in the Jhikhu Khola watershed near Dhulikhel, Nepal, has resulted in many examples of new innovations in water management. In the past ten years farmers in that watershed have changed their annual crop rotation from one to four crops. This is possible because of favorable climatic conditions, the introduction of fast-growing rice varieties, and the shift to intercropping practices. These rotation systems are now considered to be some of the most intensively cultivated plots on Earth, and one can't help but wonder how much more the farmers can push their system. There is growing evidence that many practices are not sustainable; it is becoming more difficult to maintain a balanced nutrient supply in the soils, stream water availability for irrigation has dropped in the dry season, and water pollution is now widespread.

To counter the water scarcity, farmers were introduced to the concept of water harvesting, wherein surplus water during the monsoon season is gathered in simple runoff-collection systems and then used during the dry season in combination with low-cost drip irrigation. Growing cash crops during the dry season is highly profitable, and farmers have quickly accepted and modified these techniques to improve their production capacity. The low-cost drip system, costing approximately $20 and capable of irrigating plots of over 4,000 square feet, requires little labor, uses small amounts of water, and reduces the need for applying large quantities of water-polluting fertilizers in one or two annual applications.[4]

The capacity of mountain farmers to adapt to new technologies is impressive, but the sustainability of such intense land use is worrying. Farmers in these remote areas do not have access to scientific data. Although they continually conduct experiments and come up with innovative adaptation methods, these experiments take time, and many of the problems are visible only over time.

Agriculture is not only the most water-demanding industry, but is also emerging as the largest contributor of nonpoint source pollution. The problem relates primarily to excess nutrients that are being applied to the soil in the form of fertilizer and manure, leading to eutrophication (excessive blooms of blue- green algae). Because phosphorus is usually a deficient nutrient in freshwater systems, once it is added in large quantities, the blue-green algae outcompete other organisms. As the organic matter settles and decomposition occurs, dissolved oxygen in the water reaches levels that are lethal to fish, and anoxic conditions can lead to health problems for human and aquatic organisms. Lowland areas are much more prone to increased concentrations of pollutants due to cumulative effects. It is the fresh water flowing from the mountains that helps to dilute the lowland contaminants. As animal-stocking densities are increased in the mountains to satisfy lowland meat and milk demands, water pollution is added to water sources. The soils become saturated with nutrients, most of which eventually leach into the streams. This affects the local mountain communities as well as the downstream users.

The challenge for external experts is to anticipate these problems—soil acidification, nutrient deficiencies, water pollution—and work in a preventive manner. The flow of useful information to the farmers must be improved.

Pressure does not stem only from agriculture, since tourism and hydropower generation also compete for water. The largest emerging demand for water is from mass tourism in the mountains, and the water issues associated with mountain tourism are complex. Tourism is the fastest-growing and largest industry in the world, and as beaches become more crowded, mountains become more attractive places for people to escape from urban congestion.[5] A new spirit of adventure lures people into mountains for winter sports. Urbanites seeking invigorating scenery invade mountain villages for short periods of time during the winter and summer seasons. The most intensely visited period in the alpine region extends from December to February, coinciding with minimum stream flow. This places an enormous strain on water suppliers and wastewater-treatment plants. Tourists use far more water than local residents, and consumption estimates often reach 80 to 100 gallons per person per day as opposed to more normal consumption rates of 40 to 50 gallons per person per day, and as low as 13 gallons a day in rural mountain villages.

Snowmaking, a rapidly expanding industry in many ski areas, is creating a new set of water problems. It has been estimated by Althea O'Donnell that 300 million to 400 million gallons of water are used for snowmaking in typical mountain regions. Many ski resorts built over the past 20 years are located at relatively low elevations, and the risk of low snow years coinciding with important sporting events is overcome simply by increasing the snowmaking capacity. The impact of global warming on snowmaking is a scenario that few people have contemplated. It is interesting, and perhaps unfortunate, that technology has been developed to create snow for fun and frolic rather than to retain and store water for food security and other essential services in dry mountain regions. The growing desire for year-round skiing has created even greater pressures in the ski resorts of the Southern Hemisphere (Chile, Argentina, and Peru), and similar water-management concerns are emerging in these mountain areas.

Summer recreation in the mountains has enormous implications for water managers. In areas where streams are not glacier fed, late summer stream flows are often critical for fish survival and downstream irrigation. This is the very best time for tourism, but it is also the critical time for aquatic biota. With low water levels, pollutant concentrations usually increase, putting extra stress on fish and environmental services. Golf is one of the fastest-growing recreational activities; huge quantities of water are needed to keep those courses green. Depending on the climatic regime, a typical golf course uses about 125,000 cubic feet of water per day.[6] In a summer mountain season that lasts 100 days, one green golf course could use an amount that would supply sufficient water for 6,000 people for an entire year!

Although such water-hungry activities are causes for concern, the sheer volume of tourists flocking into the mountains is alarming. Approximately 20,000 tourists visit Everest Base Camp every year.[7] Given the rapid economic growth and liberalization in China, tourism is growing at rates never imagined ten years ago. Some five million tourists now annually flock to Lijiang, a United Nations-declared heritage site near the Snowy Mountains in Yunnan. The Chinese have succeeded admirably in building the hotel infrastructure to deal with this type of tourism. Most of the visitors come from urban centers seeking a wonderful culinary experience sitting along the channeled waterways that pass through the city, with the Snowy Mountains as a backdrop. The mountain water that enters the city is refreshingly clean and turbulent—but the picture changes dramatically a few miles downstream of the city, where the cumulative effects of such mass tourism provide a sharp contrast. It remains to be seen what this influx of humanity will do to the hydrologic capacity of this mountain region.

Pilgrimages are another form of tourist stress.[8] More than nine million people descend upon a few key mountain regions in northern India each year for spiritual enlightenment. The Indian shrine at Badrinath, at 10,000 feet (over 3,000 meters), attracts half a million visitors each year. The challenge is even more dramatic since these pilgrimages occur during the few months of the year when the climatic conditions are tolerable. It's not simply pressure on water; it is a complex package of pressures that includes the entire fragile mountain ecosystem: biodiversity, firewood consumption, plant and soil ecology. Any changes in surface characteristics have a gigantic impact on the hydrologic cycle, but little attention has been given to determining how soil compaction and vegetation changes will affect water infiltration and surface runoff. Concerted efforts involving religious leaders to plant trees and rehabilitate forests have not been very successful due to the harsh winters and the very short growing season.

Some of the best communication and navigation tools in these remote mountain regions have been introduced by climbers. Those who ascend to the many Himalayan peaks are eager to communicate their accomplishments with the people back home. They bring the most sophisticated portable systems to the mountains, allowing them to communicate globally by radio, e-mail, fax, and telephone. Unfortunately, little of this technology is left behind. Perhaps these tools could be used in a more effective way to provide education and transfer knowledge that helps improve the livelihood and food security in these mountain communities. Some of this technology transfer is slowly taking place in the Everest region, where efforts have been made not only to improve rescue operations, but also to improve the communication within the medical health system. As an example, the Inventa Everest 2000 Environmental Expedition introduced water-quality monitoring technologies that are helping local communities to improve water safety and health in the Khumbu region of Nepal.

For many poor countries located in mountains, the only hope for development is to tap water and hydropower resources for export to lowland communities. This is nowhere more apparent than in the Himalayan regions, where countries like Bhutan, Nepal, and Laos are placing great hope in converting their blue resource into gold. History has not been kind to these mountain countries; relatively few water-related benefits have flown back to the mountains, and negotiations between the small countries and their large and more powerful neighbors have not been easy. Long-term commitments and agreements are needed, and far-reaching economic projections of the benefits and costs of large hydropower projects have not proved to be accurate to this point.[9] Some dams are now being demolished because they have become old and inefficient due to massive amounts of accumulated sediments. Phosphorus, which is highly insoluble, preferentially attaches itself to sediment that is detained within the reservoirs. This results in nutrient depletion below the reservoirs, which reduces the production of organisms and plants that form part of the food chain for fish. The end result is a decline in fish populations.[10] Most of these dams were built between 1950 and 1970, when there were no concerns over fish migration and ecological services, and when the demands on water for recreation, irrigation, industrial, and domestic use were low.

Hydropower companies have traditionally used water for maximizing energy production with little consideration for other water users. Now they have to learn how to share water with all other users whose demands are increasing. British Columbia Hydro, which operates one of the largest hydro systems in the world, is for the first time developing water-user plans that accommodate other users as well as maintaining fixed minimum water flow levels for the environmental services during the dry season. Developing water-reallocation plans is not easy, because it inevitably results in large economic losses to the power companies.

Since water demands are increasing and the impact of water pollution is growing, all projections point toward a water crisis in the near future. To prevent it, a concerted effort needs to be made to reduce consumption, prevent further deterioration of water quality, initiate innovative action to improve the management of water, and protect the water sources in the mountains.

What does the future hold for the 700 million people who live, mostly in poverty, in the world's most isolated mountain regions? The population diversity is large, the economic opportunities are limited, and the problems of food security are widespread. Mountain farming is risky at best, because the labor requirements are huge. Yields can never match those in lowland areas, where warmer temperatures, longer growing seasons, and richer soil conditions are more favorable. To add to the problems, markets are distant, and transportation and access are difficult.

As the discrepancy between urban demand and rural mountain poverty increases, two conflicts are emerging. The first is out-migration of working males, which increases the workload of the women who are left behind to run the farms. The second, and related, problem is that most of the mountain migrants move to cities, where they add to urban poverty. This trend is particularly evident in the Andes. Due to their isolation, mountains also easily become areas of conflict and secure havens for guerrilla movement, as seen in Afghanistan, Colombia, Peru, Kashmir, Ethiopia, and Nepal.

Addressing the economic roots of these problems is critical to establishing security and reducing risks of conflicts. To this point, mountain people have not benefited much from all the hydropower developed in their backyard. Some of these benefits must flow back from the urban centers to the mountains. Establishing water supplies in the mountains for distant use in urban centers should have provisions for a reverse flow of benefits. These promising economic tools could go a long way to assuring mountain people that there is a future in the mountains and opportunities to improve their livelihood.

Mountain communities are often thought of as conservative and traditional because of their isolation and lack of educational opportunities, but this is simply not true. There is much to be learned from the ingenuity of mountain people. They survive under the most extreme conditions, they are great risk takers, and they are relentless in their efforts to overcome the harsh conditions they live in.

There are some bright skies on the mountain horizons, and education is the key. For the first time in history their isolation is shrinking with increased access to the information technology tools that are now reaching many remote communities. The use of these tools can improve communication, give mountain communities access to education programs, and facilitate the distribution of extension service information. Tourism is playing a positive role in bringing these tools to the mountains, including those provided by climbers who infiltrate the most remote mountain regions. A very exciting component is that it is now possible to access some of the best educational programs via long-distance technologies, and mountain people can benefit greatly from this innovation.

Four Internet-based, watershed-management teaching courses offered by the University of British Columbia have reached individuals and groups of young scientists in remote areas of Bhutan, China, Cambodia, Nepal, the Philippines, and Colombia. As these scientists interact with students around the world, they gain a greater awareness about water-demand problems, water pollution, and climate change in the lowlands. At the same time, they are able to share their specific problems and solutions with others.

Education is clearly the most effective first step in addressing the water problems facing the world, and there is reason for optimism that, with these new communication tools, mountain depopulation and conflicts can be averted. At the same time, greater understanding can be gained on how to manage mountain water towers more effectively for greater social and environmental equity in the world.

CONFLICT

CONFLICT AND COOPERATION

Over the past 50 years, Israel and its neighbors have undergone a greater number of distinct water conflicts than any other region, as more and more of the Jordan River has been diverted for human use.

The breakup of the Soviet Union instantly created several new international river basins, resulting in new challenges for managing water disputes. Examples include the Kura-Araks river system, which runs through the politically volatile Caucasus region. Pollution and projected water shortages put the basin at risk for future conflicts.

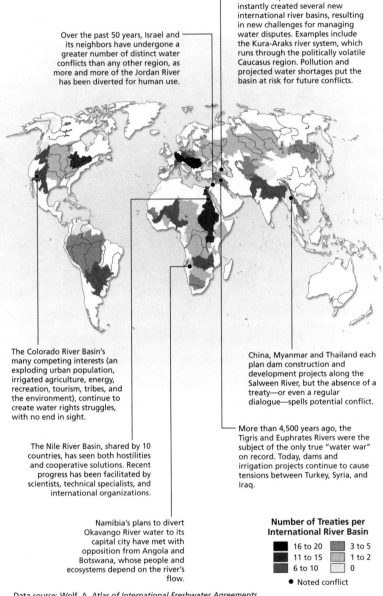

The Colorado River Basin's many competing interests (an exploding urban population, irrigated agriculture, energy, recreation, tourism, tribes, and the environment), continue to create water rights struggles, with no end in sight.

China, Myanmar and Thailand each plan dam construction and development projects along the Salween River, but the absence of a treaty—or even a regular dialogue—spells potential conflict.

The Nile River Basin, shared by 10 countries, has seen both hostilities and cooperative solutions. Recent progress has been facilitated by scientists, technical specialists, and international organizations.

More than 4,500 years ago, the Tigris and Euphrates Rivers were the subject of the only true "water war" on record. Today, dams and irrigation projects continue to cause tensions between Turkey, Syria, and Iraq.

Namibia's plans to divert Okavango River water to its capital city have met with opposition from Angola and Botswana, whose people and ecosystems depend on the river's flow.

Number of Treaties per International River Basin

- 16 to 20
- 11 to 15
- 6 to 10
- 3 to 5
- 1 to 2
- 0
- ● Noted conflict

Data source: Wolf, A. *Atlas of International Freshwater Agreements.*

I n the summer of 2001, the tiny town of Klamath Falls,
Oregon, was ablaze with discontent. For decades the surrounding valley had been made fertile by the Bureau of
Reclamation, with waters from the Klamath River rechanneled
to irrigate 200,000 acres of what would otherwise have
been arid land. But in this summer, at a time of record drought,
the federal government had cut off the water. Under federal law,
a fish—the endangered sucker fish—had first claim on the water
that hundreds of farmers like Rob Crawford had counted on.

"We're real people here, and we're being annihilated," he said in rage and despair that summer, pointing to fields that were little more than cracked earth and weeds.

The next year the government tried a different tack. It rewrote the rules governing water flows from the Klamath to allow the farmers more water, ostensibly without causing harm to the fish. But this time, instead of parched fields, the impact showed up in dead fish, with some 20,000 dead salmon turning up downriver. Though the cause was never proved beyond dispute, fishermen and environmentalists said that the farmers' victory had brought about the salmon's end.

Mark Twain, that 19th-century great, wrote so famously, "Whiskey is for drinkin'; water is for fightin'," a reminder that conflicts over water are not new. But the battle over the Klamath, one that is still unresolved, has set a particularly unsettling tone. If water is becoming increasingly scarce, will battles over water become increasingly common, whether between neighbors, farms and cities, man and beast, or even countries? If choices must be made, how can governments hope to choose between rival users, such as Mr. Crawford and a fish? And what can be done when the conflicts over water pit state against state or even country against country, as they do increasingly around the world? Are such battles likely to grow sharper as water becomes more scarce, or might the shock of shortages actually impel greater cooperation?

These are some of the questions explored in the essays that follow, which address conflicts over water at three different levels. Mike Dombeck shows how development affects water supplies by shrinking the size of forests. David J. Hayes examines the

Colorado River and the battle to reallocate water rights between farm and cities. Aaron T. Wolf writes about the Jordan River, a subject of clashes between countries and a test case for the popular view that the century ahead will include wars over water.

On that subject, of course, as well as the broader question of how water conflicts can be resolved, the jury is still out. Certainly, the potential for more battles like the one over the Klamath increases every day. Consider, for example, the case of Albuquerque, New Mexico, whose plans for a future municipal water supply have become hostage to the fate of another endangered fish, the silvery minnow of the Rio Grande. Consider southern China, whose residents stand to lose out in an enormous way to a vast government scheme to channel rivers hundreds of miles northward to the arid plains. Consider the battle between the states of Maryland and Virginia, both relatively water rich, but so worried about a water-poor future that they have taken their centuries-old dispute over the boundaries of the Potomac River to the Supreme Court. Consider Mexico, just one of many downriver countries whose supplies of water are being overtapped by an upriver neighbor, in this case the United States.

These are battles over water, but they are also battles over priorities. Is it still reasonable to guarantee, under the Endangered Species Act, that certain plants and animals have a higher claim than humans? At what point should farmers' water use give way to cities and suburban lawns? Should the sharing of a waterway give all parties a voice in others' decisions about how to use it?

One dispute entangled in these questions and more involves Atlanta and its suburbs, whose dizzying growth is seen by

Georgia's neighbors as a threat. Even in a generally rainy climate, Atlanta's water needs have begun to threaten the flow of the Chattahoochee and Apalachicola Rivers, but years of negotiations between the governors of Georgia, Florida, and Alabama have yet to produce a compromise that would satisfy Atlanta, the region's farmers, and the ecological needs of the rivers and Apalachicola Bay, a rich fishery in the Gulf of Mexico.

Is there any reason for optimism, there or anywhere else? Mr. Wolf points out that the institutions most threatened by water scarcity are the ones that have best equipped to negotiate solutions. Certainly, when the price is right, or the pressure great enough, or the alternatives sufficiently unpalatable, deals over water are struck all the time, whether it is a sale of rights by a farmer to a city or an accommodation spelled out in a treaty, such as the 1994 peace accord between Israel and Jordan. With only a few exceptions, most countries in the world have committed themselves to the principle that international water resources must be shared on an equitable basis, rather than divvied up by some equation of power.

Yet what happens when limited resources can be stretched only so far, when there is no alternative? In Klamath Falls, anger and desperation for water impelled ordinarily law-abiding farmers to take blowtorches to the floodgates so that the water they saw as theirs could flow again. In that case, the fish could not fight back. If people had been the losers, the story would have been very different. Inevitably, and repeatedly, they will be, and these conflicts will be far harder to put to rest.

"WATER WARS"

AND OTHER TALES OF HYDROMYTHOLOGY

Aaron T. Wolf

n 1978 the Dead Sea turned over for the first time in centuries. For millennia this lake at the lowest point on the Earth's surface had been receiving the sweet waters of the Jordan River, losing only pure water to relentless evaporation, and collecting the salts left behind. The result had been an inhospitably briny lake eight times saltier than the ocean, topped by a thin layer of the Jordan's relatively less dense fresh water. The two salinity levels of the river and the lake kept the Dead Sea in a perpetually layered state even while the lake level remained fairly constant—evaporation from the lake surface occurs at roughly the rate of the natural flow of the Jordan and other tributaries and springs.

This delicate equilibrium was disrupted as modern nations—with all of their human and economic needs tied inexorably to the local supply of fresh water—built up along the shores of the Jordan. In this century, both Jews and Arabs focused on this historic strip of land, with the two peoples locked in a demographic race for numerical superiority. As more and more of the Jordan was diverted for the needs of these new nations—Jordan, Syria, and Lebanon, as well as Israel—the level of the lake began to fall, most recently by about one-half meter per year. Greater amounts of the shoreline were exposed, the lake was cut in half by the Lisan Straits, the shallow southern half all but dried up, and the potash works and health spas built to take advantage of the lake's unique waters found themselves ever farther from the shore.

Along with the drop in lake level came a relative rise in the pycnocline, the dividing line between the less saline surface water and its hypersaline fossil base. The division between the two layers was finally eradicated briefly in the winter of 1978-79, and the Dead Sea turned over, effectively rolling in its grave—a hydrologic protest against the loss of the Jordan River's flow. The turnover brought water to the surface that had not seen the light of day for 300 years. Although it sterilized the lake, this turnover was not counted as an ecological disaster—except for bacteria and one type of alga, the Dead Sea is appropriately named—but the event was a symptom of a wider crisis of history-influencing proportions.

The world is running out of "easy" water, and nowhere are the shortages more acute than in the Middle East. Jordan in particular ranks high on any list of countries facing water scarcity, as do the Palestinian areas of the West Bank and Gaza, whose access to adequate water is still closely controlled by Israel and has not yet been guaranteed as part of any peace treaty. Over the past 50 years, most of the international conflicts over water have taken place between Israel and at least one of its neighbors (although the last was in 1970). In the Jordan River Basin, for example, violence broke out in the mid-1960s over an "all-Arab" plan to divert the river's headwaters (itself a preemptive move to thwart Israel's intention to siphon water from the Sea of Galilee). Israel and Syria sporadically exchanged fire between March 1965 and July 1966, and the water-related tensions in the basin have only recently begun to dissipate.

The origins of the Jordan lie near where Lebanon, Syria, Jordan, and Israel come together, and the rivalry over its waters tells us much about the difficulty of dividing water across political lines. The process of carving modern borders out of what was the Ottoman Empire dates to the end of the First World War, and, particularly in the area around the Jordan headwaters, those struggles remind us just how crucial to the debate the issue of water resources has been. From the Sykes-Picot agreement to the Paris Peace Talks, through five Arab-Israeli wars and consequent armistice arrangements, and now today's bilateral peace negotiations, the question of what will replace what was once a single entity and how its water will be divided remains less than fully resolved. Water was the last and most contentious issue resolved in negotiations over a 1994 peace treaty between Israel and Jordan, and was relegated to "final status" negotiations—along with other of the most difficult issues, such as Jerusalem and refugees—between Israel and the Palestinians.

Even so, an increasing awareness of water scarcity around the world has given rise to a number of theories, the product of what might be called a new hydromythology. The most prominent among them, as articulated by Ismail Serageldin, a vice president of the World Bank, holds that "the wars of the next century will be over water." Invariably, such warnings about "water wars" point to the arid and hostile Middle East as an example of a worst-case scenario, in part because armies have in fact been mobilized and shots fired over this scarce and precious resource.

Given that water is a vital resource for which there is no substitute, and one that ignores political boundaries and has conflicting demands on its use, it is little wonder that water is being portrayed not only as a cause of armed conflict in the past, but as the resource that will bring combatants to the battlefield in the 21st century. In the international realm, these problems are compounded by the fact that the international law governing water is poorly developed, contradictory, and unenforceable.

The only problem with the new theories is a complete lack of evidence. Although shots were fired over water between Israel and Syria in 1951-53 and 1964-66, the final exchange, including both tanks and aircraft on July 14, 1966, stopped Syrian construction of the diversion project in dispute, effectively ending water-related tensions between the two states. The 1967 war broke out almost a year later, but water had nothing to do with the strategic thinking in that Israeli-Arab conflict or those that followed in 1973 and 1982.[1]

Certainly, there is abundant and increasing potential for countries to clash over the waters they share—a group that today includes 145 nations. Of these, 21 lie in their entirety within international basins, and at least 33 countries have greater than 95 percent of their territory within these basins, meaning that they are essentially dependent for their water resources on sharing with their neighbors. These include such sizable countries as Hungary, Bangladesh, Belarus, and Zambia.[2]

The landcape of forced sharing includes 60 percent of the world's river flow and 40 percent of its population, across 263 watersheds that span the political boundaries of two or more countries.[3] This reflects a sharp increase from the 214 international basins listed in 1978,[4] the last time any official body attempted to delineate them. The increase reflects both political change (such as breakup of the Soviet Union and the Balkan states) and technological changes that have made it possible to map water resources more accurately.

Some watersheds may be particularly prone to disputes if only because of the sheer number of countries that share them. Nineteen basins are shared by five or more countries; one river, the Danube, is abutted by 17 different countries, while five more, the Congo, Niger, Nile, Rhine, and Zambezi, are shared by nine or more countries.

In order to examine more rigorously the history of water conflicts, researchers at Oregon State University undertook a three-year research project that attempted to compile a data set of *every* reported interaction between two or more nations, whether incidents of conflict or cooperation, that involved water as a scarce and/or consumable resource or as a quantity to be managed—i.e., where water is the *driver* of the events,[5] over the past 50 years.[6] The study documented more than 1,800 interactions between two or more nations over water during the past 50 years.

It reached a number of interesting conclusions. First, despite the potential for dispute in international basins, the record of acute conflict over international water resources is historically overwhelmed by the record of cooperation. As opposed to only 37 acute disputes, during this time period 157 treaties were negotiated and signed. In fact, the only true "water war" between nations on record occurred more than 4,500 years ago, between the city-states of Lagash and Umma in the Tigris-Euphrates Basin.[7]

Second, despite the fiery rhetoric of politicians, often aimed at their own constituencies rather than at the enemy, most actions taken over water are mild. Third, nations find many more issues on which to cooperate rather than fight. Fourth, water acts as both an irritant and a unifier. As an irritant, water can make good relations bad and bad relations worse, but equally, international waters can also unify basins where relatively strong institutions are in place. The historical record shows that international water disputes do get resolved, even among bitter enemies, and even as conflicts erupt over other issues. Some of the most vociferous enemies around the world have negotiated water agreements or are in the process of doing so, and the institutions they have created frequently prove to be resilient over time and during periods of otherwise strained relations. The Mekong Committee,

for example, has functioned since 1957, exchanging data throughout the Vietnam War. Secret "picnic table" talks have been held
between Israel and Jordan since the unsuccessful Johnston negotiations of 1953-55, even as these neighbors, divided by the
Jordan River, were until only recently in a legal state of war. The
Indus River Commission survived through two wars between
India and Pakistan. And all ten of the countries that share the
banks of the Nile are currently involved in negotiations over cooperative development of the basin.

So if there is little violence between nations over their
shared waters, what's the problem? Is water actually a security
concern at all? In those cases where water has caused or exac-
erbated tensions, it is worth understanding these processes to
know both how complications arise and how they are eventually resolved.

The first complicating factor is the time lag between when
nations first start to impinge on each other's water planning and
when agreements are finally, arduously reached. A general pattern
has emerged for international basins over time. Countries that share
access to a basin tend to implement water-development projects
unilaterally first on water within their territory, in attempts to avoid
the political intricacies of the shared resource. At some point, one
of the countries, generally the most powerful, will implement a
project that affects at least one of its neighbors. This project can,
in the absence of relations or institutions conducive to conflict
resolution, become a flash point, heightening tensions and regional
instability, and requiring years or, more commonly, decades to
resolve. (Treaties over the Indus took ten years of negotiations,

the Ganges thirty, and the Jordan forty.) In the meantime, water quality and quantity degrades to the point that the health of dependent populations and ecosystems is damaged or destroyed. This problem gets worse as the dispute gains in intensity; one rarely hears talk about the ecosystems of the lower Nile, the lower Jordan, or the tributaries of the Aral Sea, all of which have fallen casualty to overuse upriver and to the intractability of international disputes. During these periods, threats and disputes rage across boundaries, like those between Indians and Pakistanis and between Americans and Canadians.

Still, perhaps the more important set of disputes takes place at the subnational level. Irrigators, indigenous populations, and environmentalists, for example, can see water as tied to their very way of life, and increasingly threatened by newer uses for cities and hydropower. Numerous violent incidents have occurred at the subnational level, generally between tribes, water-use sectors, or states/provinces. In fact, our recent research at Oregon State suggests that, as the level at which a conflict is fought drops, the likelihood and intensity of violence goes up.[8] The many examples of internal water conflicts range from interstate violence and death along the Cauvery River in India, to California farmers blowing up a pipeline meant for Los Angeles, to much of the violent history in the Americas between indigenous peoples and European settlers.

As water quality degrades—or quantity diminishes—over time, the effect on the stability of a region can be unsettling. For example, for 30 years the Gaza Strip was under Israeli occupation. Water quality deteriorated steadily, saltwater intrusion degraded local wells, and water-related diseases took a rising toll on the people living there. In 1987, the *intifada*, or Palestinian uprising, broke out in the Gaza Strip and quickly spread throughout the West Bank. Was water quality the cause? It would be simplistic to claim direct causality. Was it an irritant exacerbating an already tenuous situation? Undoubtedly.

More than two-thirds of the world's water use is for agriculture, so when access to irrigation water is threatened, one result can be movement of huge populations of out-of-work, disgruntled people from the countryside to the cities—an invariable recipe for political instability. In pioneering work, Sandra Postel identified those countries that rely heavily on irrigation and whose agricultural water supplies are threatened either by a decline in quality or quantity. The list includes many of the world's current security concerns, including India, China, Pakistan, Iran, Uzbekistan, Bangladesh, Iraq, and Egypt.

A common assumption holds that scarcity of a critical resource drives people to conflict. It feels intuitive—the less there is of something, especially something as important as water, the more dear it is held and the more likely people are to fight over it. Again, though, our study at Oregon State found conclusions that were counterintuitive. Arid climates harbored no more conflicts than humid climates, and international cooperation actually *increased* during droughts. When we ran the numbers, almost no single variable proved more decisive. Democracies engaged in water conflict as often as autocracies, rich countries as often as poor countries, densely populated countries as often as sparsely populated ones, and large countries as often as small ones.

What turned out to be central was a different variable: the strength of institutions for dealing with water. Naturally arid countries were cooperative; if one lives in a water-scarce environment, one develops institutional strategies for adapting to that environment. Once we began to focus on institutions—whether defined by formal treaties, informal working groups, or generally warm relations—we began to get a clear picture of the settings most conducive to solving political tensions over international waters. What we found was that the likelihood of conflict increases significantly whenever two factors come into play. The first is that some large or rapid change occurs in the basin's physical setting—typically the construction of a dam, river diversion, or irrigation scheme—or in its political setting, especially the breakup of a nation that results in new international rivers. The second factor is that existing institutions are unable to absorb and effectively manage that change. This is typically the case when there is no treaty spelling out each nation's rights and responsibilities with regard to the shared river, or any implicit agreements or cooperative arrangements. Even the existence of technical working groups can provide some capability to manage contentious issues, as they have in the Middle East.

The overarching lesson of our study is that unilateral actions to construct a dam or river diversion in the absence of a treaty or other protective international mechanism is highly destabilizing to a region, often spurring decades of hostility before cooperation is pursued. In other words, the red flag for water-related tension between countries is not water stress per se, but rather the unilateral exercise of domination of an international river, usually by a regional power.

The scuffles over the Jordan, usually over diversion projects, are one example; another are those over the Nile, a basin shared by ten countries, with Egypt the last in line. In the late 1950s, hostilities broke out between Egypt and Sudan over Egypt's planned construction of the High Dam at Aswan. The signing of a treaty between the two countries in 1959 defused tensions before the dam was built. But even today, no water-sharing agreement exists between Egypt and Ethiopia, where some 85 percent of the Nile's flow originates, and a war of words has raged between these two nations for decades. As in the case among those who share the Jordan, the Nile nations have begun in recent years to work cooperatively toward a solution thanks in part to unofficial dialogues among scientists and technical specialists that have been held since the early 1990s, and more recently a ministerial-level "Nile Basin Initiative" facilitated by the United Nations and the World Bank.

Looking ahead, then, which river basins are ripe for conflict over the next ten years? Where are dams or diversions planned or under construction that may negatively affect other countries and where there is no mechanism for resolving resulting disputes? Our study identified 17 such basins, along with the four in which serious unresolved water disputes already exist or are being negotiated (Aral, Nile, Jordan, and Tigris-Euphrates). These basins at risk include 51 nations on five continents in just about every climatic zone. Eight of the basins are in Africa, primarily in the south, and six are in Asia, mostly in the southeast. Few of them are on the radar screens of water and security analysts.

Consider, for example, the Salween River, which rises in southern China, then flows into Myanmar (Burma) and Thailand. Each of these nations plans to construct dams and development projects along the Salween—and no two sets of plans are compatible. China, moreover, has not lately been warm to notions of water sharing. It was one of just three countries that voted against a 1997 United Nations convention that established basic guidelines and principles for the use of international rivers. Add in other destabilizing factors in the Salween Basin—including the status of Tibet, indigenous resistance movements, opium production, and a burgeoning urban population in Bangkok— and the trajectory for potential conflict begins to take shape. Without a treaty in place, or even regular dialogue among the nations about their respective plans, there is little to buffer the inevitable shock as construction begins.

Consider, too, the Okavango, the fourth largest river in southern Africa. Its watershed spans portions of Angola, Botswana, Namibia, and Zimbabwe, and its vast delta in northern Botswana offers world-renowned wildlife habitat—the "jewel of the Kalahari." In 1996, drought-prone Namibia revived colonial plans to divert Okavango water to its capital city of Windhoek. Angola and Botswana object to the scheme because of its potential harm to the people and ecosystems that depend on the Okavango's flow for their existence. The main institution that can help manage the dispute is the fledgling Okavango Commission, formed in 1994 to coordinate plans in the basin. The commission has recently received renewed support from the Southern Africa Development Community, the U.S. Bureau of

Reclamation, and other agencies, but the water dispute continues to simmer.

Several river basins are at risk of future disputes more because of rapid changes in their political settings than any specific dam or development scheme. The breakup of the Soviet Union resulted in several new international river basins almost overnight, and, not surprisingly, institutional capacity for managing water disputes in them is weak. The Kura-Araks river system, for example, runs through the politically volatile Caucasus, including the newly independent countries of Armenia, Georgia, and Azerbaijan. The river system is the source of drinking water for large portions of these nations, but millions of tons of untreated sewage and industrial waste regularly push water pollution to 10 to 100 times international standards. On top of these problems, some forecasts project severe water shortages within ten years.

At their heart, though, as with the Jordan, these are disputes over sharing something that has never been easily shared.

The Dan River, the largest source of the Jordan, emerges from five karst springs. The flow, about 250 million cubic meters per year of cool, clean water is relatively constant throughout the year, fed by rain and the melting snows of Mount Hermon, which towers above Israel's Huleh Valley. Nevertheless, in this heavy winter, the wettest in 150 years of record, the water roars and we have to shout our conversation. As one moves away from the springs, keeping careful eyes on the water-rounded basalt rocks that make up the haphazard path, one passes by the remains of an enormous pistachio tree that was used as a marker by Jewish irregulars on the route for smuggling immigrants from Syria, Iraq, and Lebanon before the state of Israel was established.[9]

Away from the water's flow, the trees thin out, the air warms the bare ground, and one's feet again kick up dust as one moves up the gentle path to Tel Dan. *Tel* is a special word particular to areas with ancient settlement. When sites particularly strategic for one reason or another are settled for so long that they rise out of the surrounding landscape, forming small but distinct hills, each layer of settlement built on the ruins of the last, the rise is called a tel. This site dates back at least through the second millennium B.C., when it served as a gateway on the Via Maris, the trade route between the two fertile crescents of antiquity along the Nile and the Euphrates. The constant source of water proved an irresistible draw to travelers making the long journey, and Dan, built in a crescent around the springs, became one of the few major urban centers in the area.[10]

The Egyptians sent out the first army to conquer the area, and were in power when Abraham and his family made their journey to Canaan, probably along the worn route of tin traders past Dan, about 2000 B.C.[11] Over time Egyptian power gave way to the Canaanites, who called the site Laish and who, in turn, ceded to the Israelite tribe of Dan about 1100 B.C. During Israelite rule, Dan prospered and it is in the remains of this period through which we walk in the lengthening shadows of late afternoon.

Inside, the stone remains of streets, a market square, and guardrooms are visible. One ascends along the ceremonial path and climbs a series of ancient stone steps to reach the most dominant spot. Stepping out onto a promontory, a clear view is gained of the springs and surrounding nature preserve. From here, one sees Mount Hermon, its snowcapped peak suggesting a distinguished head of white hair and, hence, the Druze name Jebel (Mountain) Sheikh, towering to the northwest. Between the Hermon and the Golan Heights, the plateau that creates a virtual wall of basalt along the eastern flank of the Huleh Valley, one can make out the narrow pass of the Via Maris. Here, in its isolation as the northernmost point of ancient Israel, one can almost hear in the resonance of rushing water echoes of ancient writings. Was the composer of Psalm 42, probably a priest exiled from Jerusalem, here when he wrote from "the land of Jordan, from the hills of Hermon." "As the hart yearns after the water brooks," he penned, "so yearns my soul for thee, oh Lord. Deep calls unto deep at the sounds of your waters. All Your waves and billows flow over me...."

The walls of Dan, once known as Jeroboam, did not hold back the Assyrians. Nor did their might hold back the Persians; nor theirs the Greeks, theirs the Ptolemaics, theirs the Romans. Each empire swept through Dan, each leaving a layer of history in the tel's horizontal record.

That, in any event, is the archaeological explanation for the small rise above the Dan springs, as chronicled in each layer's collection of pottery and coins.

There is another explanation, though, chronicled only in legend: The headwaters of the Jordan River were originally three separate streams flowing in various directions, and quarreling constantly over which was the largest and most important. Finally, the streams invited the Lord of the Universe to judge between them. The Lord descended and made for himself a throne, a small hill between the streams that, until today, was known as Tel Dan or Tel el-Kadi, Hill of the Judge in both Hebrew and Arabic. "Rivers! Ye are dear to Me, all three. Hearken to My counsel: Unite together and ye will indeed be the most important."

And so the Jordan River was formed...

Given the absence of the same kind of explicit divine intervention over the question of modern borders in the region, it is probably not surprising that those disputes as well as those over water have not, after 70 years of quarreling, yet been resolved. Today, just north of Tel Dan are the remains of a road that runs almost exactly east-west from Tyre to Damascus and beyond. For centuries the entire road lay under one authority—that of the Ottoman Turks. Today, the road is maintained in pieces: Tyre to Qantara in Lebanon, Qantara to Metulla in what was until recently the Israeli-occupied "security zone," Metulla to Banyas (after a sharp detour south around Lebanese territory) in Israel, Banyas to Majdal Shams in the Golan Heights, and Majdal Shams to Damascus in Syria. In these times, one cannot travel the length of the road no matter how many passports one has or which diplomatic strings one pulls. But in the wrangling that followed at the end of the First World War, it was because of French insistence on access to this road that the Jordan River watershed was drawn and quartered in a similar piecemeal fashion.

The difference is, of course, that a road divided can be rerouted. But a river divided is a dispute—and a long, circuitous process of negotiations—just waiting to happen.

FROM THE FOREST

TO THE FAUCET

Mike Dombeck

New York City has some of the best water in the world, and the reason is trees. Three forested watersheds between 25 and 125 miles from Manhattan supply remarkably clean water to more than ten million people. Because forests are good at naturally cleansing water, New York is exempt from using expensive filtration equipment. But to maintain that status (and to avoid billions of dollars in costs for building and operating a filtration plant), the Environmental Protection Agency has warned, New York must maintain the watersheds and protect the forests from excessive logging, development, and other degradation.

What really happens when we turn on the tap and water appears? Often there is a close connection between the forest and faucet. Most of the country's water comes from forestlands, serving millions of Americans. Forests cover about a third of the continental United States, but they account for about two-thirds of the runoff. The national forests alone are part of more than 3,400 municipal watersheds that serve 60 million Americans, and millions more rely on aquifers whose recharge flows from public and privately owned forests. A conservative estimate by the U.S. Forest Service in 2000 gave the value of water flowing from the national forests at 3.7 billion dollars a year.

Of course, forests are better known for timber, livestock forage, minerals, oil, and gas resources that wield considerable political muscle by highly competitive development and extractive industries. In the conflict between development and environmental quality, fresh water often loses.

In the U.S., we continue to use wood products at an alarming rate. Although our population is less than 5 percent of the world's total, we consume more than 25 percent of the industrial wood supply. From 1971 to 1996 the average size of new homes in the U.S. increased from 1,520 to 2,120 square feet despite a decrease in family size. At the same time, our overall demand for water is also growing. Water consumption doubled in the U.S. during the past 40 years, and demands for agriculture and household use continue to escalate. A typical American family of four uses about 345 gallons of water per day, as compared with only 80 gallons per day for the same size family in developing countries. Only 3 percent of U.S. household use is for cooking and drinking. High water consumption rates are compounded by the pattern of population growth, especially in the West, where already scarce water supplies are threatened.

In other parts of the world, in the tropics in particular, forests are being cleared for lumber, farming, and grazing at an alarming rate. During the past three decades, some 550,000 square kilometers, or 15 percent, of Brazil's Amazon rain forest have been deforested, as new roads bring in scores of farmers and ranchers who clear the trees. Using slash-and-burn techniques, they plant crops and raise cattle. But much of Amazonia is not suitable for this kind of agriculture because its soils quickly become leached of their nutrients under the tropical rains, and with the trees gone, nutrients are not returned to the soil through natural recycling. Within a few years the farmers and ranchers must move on and clear more land. Although most of the rivers in Amazonia are still healthy, the process is slowly beginning to take its toll.

Perhaps more important, when rain forest trees are removed, their ability to generate rain goes with them. In western Amazonia some 80 percent of the rain comes from the forest, whereas in Manaus, in the heart of the basin, about half is from the forest and half from the ocean. Near the Amazon Delta almost all of the rain comes from the ocean. When the trees are gone, the region will dry out and once again we will witness man's capacity for error.

Timber and water both come from the forests. How then can we manage forests so that both can thrive? No matter how enlightened our land-management policies are, there will be constant pressures to increase commodity production as long as the demand for forest products continues to escalate. Given scenarios like this, solutions are badly needed. A look back in time tells us that this struggle has a long history and that our abuse of the land and water carries a high price.

The planet is littered with the ruins of extinct civilizations that should remind us of our fallibility. Many places in the Old World serve as examples, including the bare rocky hills of Greece and Israel, and parts of Africa's steppes and deserts, all of which were once covered with forests and wooded savannas. The trees and shrubs were cut for fuel and cleared for farming. After centuries of unsustainable use and abuse caused by too many people pushing the land too hard, the topsoil eroded and forests were replaced with deserts. The land lost its ability to retain soil and water, water tables dropped, lakes and streams were contaminated or dried up, and deserts expanded. People could no longer survive on the land without technological support and imports of food and water. Great civilizations vanished.

Present-day Iraq, centered along the Tigris and Euphrates Rivers, contains ancient Mesopotamia, one of the great cradles of civilization. The region, also part of the Fertile Crescent, was lush agricultural land between 2,000 and 10,000 years ago. But today, due in large part to environmental mismanagement over the millennia, the region is anything but fertile. Similar destructive cycles currently threaten many parts of the world: Rich soils are becoming too salty to support agriculture, precipitation cycles are changing, water tables are falling, lakes and streams are drying up, and grasslands and former forests are slowly being transformed into deserts.

In North America, early European settlers found the New World very much to their liking. Land east of the Mississippi River had plentiful water, lush forests and grasslands with well-developed soils, and adequate precipitation throughout the year. But as the frontier expanded west, settlers encountered the progressively more arid Great Plains, followed by the arid Great Basin and the southwestern deserts, where the landscape was much less hospitable. The national government encouraged westward expansion and settlement through policies that were often based on poor information. Believing that trees would bring rainfall to arid land, Congress passed the Timber Culture Act in 1873. Under the act, citizens were given 160-acre parcels of land provided they planted 40 acres in trees spaced no more than 12 feet apart and kept them growing for ten years. In 1874 and again in 1878, amendments were passed reducing the tree-planting requirement to ten acres and to 6,750 trees, respectively.

Unfortunately, many citizens during the 1800s saw the West as a vast "garden land" where eastern farming practices, which depended on adequate and predictable rainfall, would flourish. A series of wet years following the Civil War, coupled with romanticized notions of "western gardens," led to the general perception that "rain would follow the plough." Sadly, the net effect of these policies was to lure land-hungry settlers into difficult circumstances only to find hardship and failure. The Dust Bowl of the 1930s brought drought, erosion, crop failures, parched vegetation, and desertification.

During the same period, another tragedy was unfolding east of the Mississippi River. Forests had been cleared by settlers for fuel and agriculture and by timber companies for railroad ties and lumber. The nation's prime hardwood forests of Appalachia and the great white pine forests of the Northeast and Midwest were clear-cut with no efforts at reforestation. Fires were often intentionally set on these lands to eliminate the brush and slash that remained. Many of the fires quickly burned out of control, some taking human lives and destroying thousands of forested acres, including the vegetation and valuable topsoils. Rains produced raging floods and severe soil erosion. The Peshtigo fire of 1871 in northeastern Wisconsin remains the most devastating forest fire in U.S. history, killing some 1,500 people and burning about 1.3 million acres. Fires in Michigan scorched another 2.5 million acres that same year. With vegetation destroyed and topsoil either turned to ash or washed away, the once majestic forests were decimated. Millions of acres of land lost resilience and the ability to temper floods and dampen drought. It would take many decades to restore the landscape. By 1900, 80 million acres of charred stumplands dominated much of the once majestic forests east of the mighty Mississippi River.

Early settlers used the land as they wished, generally with little concern for any of the consequences. They cleared forests, hunted indiscriminately, and dredged streams for precious metals. Later settlers began mining the bedrock in search of riches, leaving behind open scars on the landscape. Their rapacious legacy remains today. Colorado's national forests contain some 11,300 abandoned mines, 1,500 of which continue to exact an environmental toll. Mercury levels from abandoned mines in Oregon, thousands of pounds per year, have caused the state to warn people not to eat fish from 11 bodies of water. In Montana, more than a century of copper mining has created the largest Superfund site in the country along a 120-mile stretch of the Clark Fork River. The waters of many western rivers were diverted for irrigation or into canals for barges, leaving previously perennial streams dry during part of the year. Rivers were dammed and waters were impounded. Diversions dramatically altered the integrity of wetland and riverine ecosystems, created barriers to fish passage, and changed natural river dynamics.

After the Civil War, the modern conservation movement slowly began to emerge. The seminal publication of *Man and Nature* by George Perkins Marsh in 1864 influenced many early conservationists, from Theodore Roosevelt to Aldo Leopold. Carl Schurz, Secretary of the Interior from 1877 to 1881, became the first presidential Cabinet member with an active interest in natural resources conservation. He advocated the creation of forest reserves and a federal forest service. In 1891, the Forest Reserve Act was passed authorizing the President to set aside forest reserves from the public domain. A few years later the Forest Management Act or Organic Act of 1897 was passed. Based on a report by the National Academy of Sciences, the Organic Act specified that "no public forest reservation shall be established, except to improve and protect the forest within the reservation, or for the purpose of securing favorable conditions of water flows, and to furnish a continuous supply of timber...."

These laws applied mostly to the western U.S., where unsettled public lands remained; virtually all land east of the

Mississippi was privately owned. However, with the passage of the Weeks Act of 1911, the government began to purchase depleted farmsteads, cleared forestlands, and burned-over woodlands east of the Mississippi River for the purpose of "conserving the forests and the water supply." From 1911 to 1945, 24 million acres were added to the national forests east of the Great Plains. The reforestation of millions of acres of the cleared forests in the East was among the greatest conservation achievements of the last century. Although today's eastern forests pale in comparison with their historic grandeur and diversity, we now have more forested acres in the East than we had in 1900. The achievement has been nothing short of phenomenal: By allowing trees to reestablish themselves through natural ecological succession in some areas, and by actively replanting forests in others, devastated and burned-over clear-cuts with badly depleted soils have been transformed into more naturally functioning watersheds.

The remarkable achievement of reforesting much of the eastern U.S. notwithstanding, we continue to face tremendous hurdles in meeting freshwater needs and managing watersheds. Indeed, despite what we know about the interconnected nature of ecosystems and watersheds, coupled with the realization of how we negatively affected them in the past and our understanding of how to remedy problems, we now face even more daunting challenges due to population pressure and the lack of support for implementing sustainable development strategies.

The symptoms are unmistakable. The collective effect of dams, water diversions, pollution, habitat destruction, and the introduction of nonnative species has led to the imperiled status of many fish and other aquatic species. Nearly two-thirds of the nation's freshwater mussels are at risk of extinction, and almost one in ten already may have vanished forever. About half of all crayfish species are at risk of extinction, and about 35 percent to 40 percent of freshwater fishes and amphibians share the same gloomy prognosis. Many people are at least vaguely aware of the degradation of our earthly environment. We see pollution on the land, witness the loss of forests, and can testify to the spread of invasive weeds. But too often, what happens beneath the water's surface is out of sight, and therefore out of mind.

In the Rocky Mountains, in response to worsening water supply problems, some are proposing schemes that would allow logging to boost water resources. Advocates claim that clear-cutting 25 percent to 40 percent[1] of high-country forest patches will increase water yields and ease regional water shortages. The idea holds that cleared mountain slopes generate more runoff than intact forests largely because less water escapes to the atmosphere and less soaks into the ground. Thus, like a parking lot, more water runs off the land into lakes and reservoirs when it rains and when snow melts.

The idea sounds good at first, but upon careful inspection it loses its appeal. When trees are removed, water yields increase. But those increases are quickly followed by sharp decreases as young, even-age dense stands regenerate, which can persist for decades or more. Older, more natural forests, with trees of many different sizes and canopy gaps from tree falls, maintain relatively high water yields. Clear-cut forests display extreme highs and lows in water yield, with an overall lower long-term average than mature forests.

Healthy mature forests produce not only the most water but also the best water. The vegetation and plant litter on the soil surface keep water on the land longer. As water percolates through soils, it is naturally filtered. Clear-cutting forests, regardless of how carefully done, results in higher peak flows following spring thaws and heavy rains. These higher flows lead to more erosion and higher sediment loads in streams. Healthy forests are also better at maintaining the water chemistry and temperatures of streams. Clear-cuts lead to more nutrients in streams and higher summer water temperatures, which often harm native biota.

The direct costs of logging for water are also high. The never-ending cycle of cutting, sometimes applying chemicals, and clearing—again and again—is capital and labor intensive. The reservoirs needed to store the water from high-flow periods to augment the more extended low-flow periods are expensive to build and dredge. Dredging would also be needed in navigable streams and behind downstream hydroelectric dams. Water purification costs would rise due to increased sedimentation. And costly cleanups would follow the floods and landslides that would periodically arise.

We all live in a watershed; it is all the land drained by a single river system. Small watersheds drained by a single small stream are nested in larger watersheds. In simple terms, a watershed's function involves the interaction of soil, water, and vegetation. An objective of sound land-use management should be to keep water on the land longer so it has time to percolate into the soil, where it is filtered as gravity and capillary action move it ever deeper to replenish groundwater and recharge aquifers. Plants and their root systems bind the topsoil, reducing erosion. Layers of decaying vegetation and rich organic soil act as a porous sponge absorbing the rainfall. Trees reduce the effects of extreme weather events, slowing runoff and buffering winds.

Healthy rivers are products of healthy watersheds. Watersheds in good condition store and release rain and snowfall in amounts that maintain natural flow regimes. If floods occur, energy from high river flows is dispersed onto floodplains where stands of healthy riparian vegetation trap silt and dissipate energy. Water from healthy rivers connects the landscape in all directions—laterally onto riparian areas and into upland habitats. River health depends on proper conditions in upstream headwaters. If headwaters, riparian areas, and uplands stay within natural flow cycles, then downstream river, floodplain, and valley bottomlands maintain habitat diversity and complexity.

A truly healthy watershed—one that stretches from headwaters to bottomlands and groundwater to surface waters, with all elements in proper balance—is rare. Especially rare are naturally functioning valley bottomland habitats. Over time, most lower-elevation rivers, floodplains, and valley bottomlands have been simplified, fragmented, and constrained by a combination of agricultural and urban development, dams, highways, and railroads. Implicit in the concept of a healthy watershed is the integrity of the continuum of lands from headwaters to river mouths.

Today, we have a better scientific understanding of watershed processes than at any time in history. Our land-use practices have tremendously improved over the past century. But much of the science is not broadly applied. Additionally, we err in thinking that technological solutions can solve all of our problems or improve on natural processes. Leaders of the International Biome Program warned three decades ago: "Humankind's ability to modify the environment will increase faster than their ability to foresee the effects of their activities.... If it is impossible to eliminate catastrophic outcomes by anticipating them, then it is necessary to adopt a strategy which will eliminate such outcomes without the requirements of anticipation."

The first major laws concerning forest management approved about a century ago clearly called for a priority on water and watershed management. As we moved into World War II and the postwar housing boom, we also moved into our second timber harvest era with increasing demand for timber from the national forests. From the early 1940s to the 1980s, timber harvested from the national forests increased from less than three billion board feet annually to over 12 billion each year. (A board foot is a 12-inch square piece of lumber one inch thick. It takes about 15,000 board feet of lumber to build today's average three-bedroom home.) By the 1940s, much of the privately owned timber had been harvested, and the remaining old-growth timber was on federal land. In practice, during this era, virtually anything that got in the way of timber harvest was referred to as a "timber constraint." Thus, watershed concerns became a "constraint" to timber harvest.

Today, timber harvests from national forests have returned to about the pre-World War II level. Unfortunately, only a small fraction of our majestic old-growth forests remains intact. The trends in forest management are moving back to a watershed approach with a new knowledge and an emphasis on the entire ecosystem. This is good news for water and watershed health. Cities like New York that maintain close relationships with these forests are living, functioning examples of these benefits.

Almost half a century ago we got our first glimpse of Earth from outer space. The powerful images depicted with crystal clarity what we already knew but had never seen—the majesty of Earth's watery splendor. From the deep blue seas to the shroud of clouds, water dominates the planet. Despite this abundance, we struggle to meet our freshwater needs.

Forests cannot be all things to all people all the time. Inevitably, as managers in the United States and around the world try to manage them for all uses, conflicts will arise. But water is perhaps the most undervalued and underappreciated forest product. If the goal of forest management should be to secure the "greatest good for the greatest number, for the longest time," as envisioned by the first U.S. Forest Service chief Gifford Pinchot, today there can be no higher priority than to do everything possible to allow forests to optimally generate life-giving water.

ACCOMMODATION TURNS TO CONFLICT:

LESSONS FROM THE COLORADO

David J. Hayes

With his cowboy hat and crusty manner, Lloyd Allen, a farmer in California's Imperial Valley, did not look like a water baron. But in the poker-table atmosphere around the negotiating table, Mr. Allen had the best hand in the deck. Once again, with the help of federal, state, and local officials, California was trying to divide its water resources between farms and cities. But this time, in the late 1990s, in negotiations that began in 1999, a solution was proving evasive.

Across the table from Allen were the Imperial Valley's usual protagonists—the Coachella Valley Water District negotiators from the neighboring Palm Springs area, whom Allen resented for their glitter and golf courses. And the hosts of the meeting, the sophisticated and urbane Ron Gastelum and his fellow brass at the Metropolitan Water Authority of Southern California, ensconced in their angular, glass-and-steel high-rise in downtown Los Angeles, were light-years removed from the dusty towns of Brawley and El Centro that Allen and his fellow negotiators called home.

Allen and other elected leaders of the Imperial Irrigation District were toeing a treacherous line. They could not be seen as selling off their water rights to the cities. Water rights were synonymous with the Imperial Valley's proud farming heritage and were widely viewed as central to their way of life. Selling water to voracious cities looked like selling out—regardless of price. It was not a comfortable position for an elected member of the Water District.

At the same time, with first call on more than 75 percent of the state of California's entire allocation of Colorado River water, Allen knew that everyone else around the table coveted Imperial's water. He knew that it was better to cut a deal with the cities, so long as he made it clear that it was Imperial who was setting the terms. Allen's blood pressure rose with threats by city interests to investigate whether the farmers were using their prodigious water supply carefully, or whether they were violating their covenant not to waste any of the water that the feds were giving them at virtually no cost. If Imperial was going to sell some of its vast supply of Colorado River water to the fast-growing, water-starved cities on the California coast, as just about everyone else believed was prudent, Allen and the others would need to decide that it was worth their while.

Mark Twain famously declared, "Whiskey is for drinkin'; water is for fightin'." But over the past century, and at least until a few years ago, the real story of water has been one of accommodation: the use of political power and creative dealmaking to stretch limited supplies and avoid conflict. When early pioneers recognized that the lack of water might retard development of the West, it was lawyers and not gunslingers who swung into action. Young states and territories simply changed the law, developing a revolutionary new legal system that gave the best rights to those who would put the water to use first—for mining, ranching, or irrigation.

When legal changes were not enough, new infrastructure was built to "create" new sources of reliable water. By the middle of the 20th century, when a second wave of settlers bumped up against physical limitations, rugged individualism yielded to governmental largesse with the appropriation of huge federal investments in water infrastructure to stretch native water supplies. As described by author Marc Reisner, a "Cadillac Desert" of wildly ambitious projects was conceived, and then implemented, in a period that stretched into the 1970s. The country's largest river systems were reengineered into water-storage and water-delivery systems, providing steady, strong flows of water year-round to urban and rural users alike.

In many water basins in the West, however, there are no longer any easy answers to accelerating water demands. No other river system illustrates the point better than the Colorado River—arguably the most important single water source in the U.S. The Colorado is not a mighty river in terms of quantity; its annual flow averages only one-tenth the flow of the Pacific Northwest's Columbia River. But over its 1,700-mile length, it drains 246,500 square miles in seven states, one-twelfth of the continental United States. Most important, the Colorado River is the primary water source for much of the arid and semiarid Southwest. It is the water lifeline for the fastest growing states in the union, including Utah, Colorado, New Mexico, Arizona, Nevada, and California.

Historically, management of the Colorado River was relatively easy. A small group of interested parties headed off future conflicts by making sensible, and relatively painless, accommodations. When Californians first proposed building the Hoover Dam to control devastating floods on the lower Colorado, for example, the other basin states resisted. They feared that a controlled river would facilitate more water use in California (as, in fact, it later did), creating a danger that the state would use the prior appropriation doctrine, which gives priority in water disputes to the earliest users, as a sword to claim more Colorado River water as its own.

Rather than fight, the states compromised. With Herbert Hoover presiding, the upper and lower basin states agreed to split overall water rights in the Colorado, with each basin having rights to 7.5 million acre feet of water. Later, the lower basin states took the next step and divided their water rights among Nevada, Arizona, and California. This was yet another accommodation made relatively easy by the fact that the states were dividing up waters that they never thought they would be able to use, as illustrated by Nevada's willingness to settle for an allocation of only 300,000 acre feet, while its more farsighted neighbors Arizona and California netted many multiples of that—2.8 and 4.4 million acre foot allocations, respectively.

Likewise, dividing up Colorado River water within each state was relatively easy, early on. Within California, four of the primary users of Colorado River water simply agreed among themselves in the late 1920s to take the lion's share of the water, with the predominant agricultural districts being the big winners. Specifically, the Imperial Irrigation District, representing water users in the Imperial Valley, agreed to share a total of 3.85 million acre feet with three other agricultural districts, all of which were smaller. Imperial later cut a deal with the next biggest agricultural water district, the Coachella Valley Water District, representing users in the Palm Springs area, to subordinate Coachella's priority, essentially giving Imperial Valley first call on well more than three million acre feet of water—more than the entire allocation for the state of Arizona.

Urban water users were not a major factor in the 1920s when California divvied up its 4.4 million acre feet of Colorado River water. Los Angeles's Metropolitan Water District was assured less than one-quarter of the water due to California in normal years—only 550,000 acre feet of the state's 4.4 million acre feet. In 1930, however, L.A.'s population was less than two million people, and it had just bought up another water supply in Owens Valley in the Sierras. Los Angeles had no apparent water worries. As a result,

DAVID J. HAYES / 143

the deal was cut among the agencies with a minimum of discussion, and California summarily adopted it as the state's policy, without questioning the private allocation of its water resources.

There were controversies, to be sure, associated with the early decisions that carved up the Colorado, including some colorful ones. Arizona periodically threw a tantrum, acting out its paranoia that downstream California would somehow take all of its water. After agreeing to a split of Colorado River water in 1922, for example, Arizona had second thoughts, refusing for the next two decades to ratify its interstate compact with California and Nevada, and choosing instead to snipe at California at every turn. In 1934, Arizona went so far as to attempt to halt construction of Parker Dam, the turnout for the new Colorado River Aqueduct that would deliver water to Los Angeles. Arizona's Governor B.B. Moeur ordered six members of the Arizona National Guard to travel to Parker, Arizona, and to report back on "any attempt on the part of any person to place any structure on Arizona soil either within the bed of said river or on the shore." Later, when a trestle bridge was being built toward the Arizona shore, more than a hundred guardsmen were brought in "to repel an invasion." The would-be combatants were called off when President Roosevelt bribed Arizona into submission by agreeing to more federal pork in the form of a federal investment in the Gila Project, a large irrigation project in central Arizona.

Arizona finally ratified the Colorado River Compact in 1944 in order to protect its water supply from an impending treaty between the United States and Mexico. Arizona continued to look out for its own interests, however, as its leaders pushed hard—decade after decade—for federal support for a massive delivery system that would bring its water deep into the center of the state. The other basin states objected but, in typical Colorado River fashion, a compromise was reached. Arizona agreed that it would be shorted first during times of drought so long as the feds and other basin states, through their congressional representatives, agreed to finance the four-billion-dollar Central Arizona Project. The other basin states put forward their projects, including Colorado's infamous Animas La Plata Project and New Mexico's San Chama Project—a transbasin diversion that Albuquerque is counting on today to bail it out of a serious water-supply problem. Having scratched the itches of the then-ascendant interests on the river, Congress finally authorized the construction of the Central Arizona Project in 1968.

Colorado River history buffs treat these sources of conflict on the river as epic struggles. Each situation presented serious issues, to be sure, but with a limited field of interested players (primarily, the states themselves), the would-be protagonists always developed accommodations that left all parties satisfied. And through all the negotiations, individual water users within basin states never seemed to be at risk. The "Law of the River" was formed by compromises that flowed from frictions among—and rarely within—the basin states.

Today's crisis presents wholly different challenges that illustrate the shift from accommodation to conflict that marks water issues throughout the West. Fundamental changes in demographics, culture, and values are coming to the fore at the same time that the traditional tools for brokering conflicting water needs are on the wane.

The biggest change, of course, is the massive shift in population to the cities served by the Colorado River. The river used to meander through John Wesley Powell's desolate "Great American Desert." Today, Colorado's upstream tributaries provide much of the water that sustains a growing metropolis in Denver and which a water-constrained Albuquerque is counting on for its long-term water supply. In its middle reaches, the Colorado services the booming desert cities of Phoenix, Tucson, and Las Vegas. And before it crosses the Mexican border, the Colorado supplies 19 million southern Californians in Los Angeles, Orange County, and San Diego with fully a third of their water needs. That's approximately 25 million Americans in metropolitan areas who need the Colorado River to keep the taps turned on.

In addition to creating new demands on supply, the cities have introduced a new factor in the water world—money, and lots of it. With 19 million customers, the Metropolitan Water District of Southern California can support a billion-dollar-a-year construction budget without difficulty. And the "Met" certainly has no problem buying water if it's available. Ditto for the metropolises of Las Vegas, San Diego, and Phoenix. With their massive customer bases, urban water costs in the Los Angeles area of $300 or $400 per acre foot barely raise an eyebrow. In contrast, Lloyd Allen and his fellow Imperial Valley farmers pay only $15 per acre foot for Colorado River water. A five-dollar surcharge on an Imperial water bill would represent a 30 percent increase in the price of irrigation water; Imperial constituents would have none of it, even though they are shipping out one billion dollars in agricultural goods each year.

Money has changed the whole game. Many of the farmers in Palo Verde Irrigation District—which also is served by the Colorado—have been only too happy to enter into a deal with the Met. The Palo Verde farmers sell their water during dry periods when Los Angeles needs it most, while they happily take a Met-financed vacation. Many growers in the Imperial Valley also are enticed by the prospect of being paid by their thirsty city neighbors not to farm, but the predominant view in the valley is sharply critical of the potential negative impacts on the valley's farming heritage and its employment base if some lands become fallow to free up water for sale to the cities. That's why Lloyd Allen has such a tough job. Selling Imperial Valley water on a profit margin of more than 2,000 percent wouldn't be so hard if it weren't for culture, tradition, and the ever present fear that Imperial Valley will become the next dried-up Owens Valley of "Chinatown" fame.

In addition to the changes wrought by the rise of the cities, with their full pocketbooks, the Colorado's water issues have become more complicated still by the emergence of difficult new issues and constituencies in recent years. At the top of everyone's list is the environment. Engineered changes on the river have had a devastating impact on Colorado's native fish, who knew a less channeled, siltier river that was not punctuated by large, languid lakes. Birds also have suffered with the loss of flood-induced habitat, with the largest losses occurring in the dried-up Colorado River Delta in Mexico—

once a hotspot for wildlife and now a struggling shadow of its former self.

Even the unattractive Salton Sea has become environmentally important. The sea owes its creation, and continued existence, to the Colorado River. It was originally formed when one of the Colorado's periodic floods roared through early Imperial Valley irrigation works in 1905 and burst through the canal, pulling the entire flow of the Colorado River into a low spot north of Imperial Valley. Within a short, two-year period, the Colorado formed California's largest inland body of water—the Salton Sea. Repairs that were hailed as one of the most significant engineering feats of the day restored the Colorado to its original channel in 1907, leaving the Salton Sea behind as a reminder of the power of the Colorado. The Salton Sea continues to be sustained, to this day, largely by Colorado River runoff from irrigated fields in the Coachella and Imperial Valleys.

Although the Salton Sea was created by an accident of man, it now plays a unique role in the region as one of the few significant remaining stopovers for migratory birds on the Pacific flyway. More than 400 species of birds visit the Salton Sea—including the endangered brown pelican and Yuma clapper rail and 50 percent of the entire population of the eared grebe—feasting on a fishery that Dr. Milt Friend of the United States Geological Survey has characterized as one of the most productive on Earth.

The river also attracts a large, and growing, tourism economy built around the many national parks, monuments, and recreational areas in the Colorado River Basin, including massive

Lake Mead and Lake Powell, which were formed by the Hoover and Glen Canyon dams. These large bodies of water have spawned a huge, water-based recreational industry in the midst of one of the driest areas of the nation. And sandwiched between the houseboats and water sports on the two vast lakes is a stretch of the Colorado that winds through the incomparable Grand Canyon, attracting five million visitors each year.

That doesn't include the many Native Americans who call the Colorado Basin their home. For centuries the mysterious Anasazi lived alongside the Colorado and its tributaries before suddenly vanishing more than a thousand years ago. Today, dozens of tribes, from the Havasupai and the Hualapai to the Navajo and Hopi, have their homeland in the basin, and have strong spiritual, and legal, connections with the river. The Hopi, for example, want to use Colorado River water to replace groundwater that currently is used in connection with coal mining on their reservation, and the Navajo recently filed a major new federal court suit claiming rights to significant flows on the Colorado. And the San Luis Rey Band of Indians in California have been looking for years to secure their early water rights via an award of Colorado River water.

All of these conflicting factors bring us back to the bargaining table where Lloyd Allen, Ron Gastelum, and others are squaring off, seeking to sort through the difficult legal, cultural, and financial terms of a potential water transfer, while struggling with complications brought on by emerging environmental issues and outstanding Indian claims.

If it is so tough to do a deal, why not just walk away? What is keeping Allen, Gastelum, and the others at the table, month after month, year after year, trying to find a way to transfer a modest amount of water from the Imperial Valley to San Diego?

The decisions made years ago have run up against the basin's striking new demographics. In 1922, California agreed to cap its Colorado River water use at the then-fantastic level of 4.4 million acre feet in a normal year. An additional agreement in 1929 divided up the 4.4-million-acre-feet supply, with 3.85 million going to agricultural users and the balance going to the Los Angeles urban community—in line with the view that superior rights should be granted to the early users of water, the pioneer desert irrigators.

These early accommodations held, with little controversy, for many decades. Even when California's water use continued to expand up to the 4.4-million-acre-foot allocation, and then beyond, neither Nevada nor Arizona was using its legal entitlement. California had plenty of additional lower basin water to take off the river, without harm to anyone.

All that changed by the mid 1990s with the completion of the Central Arizona Project and the explosive growth of Las Vegas and southern Nevada. Nevada soon ran out of its limited Colorado River water supply. And once the Arizona project came on-line, the state suddenly became physically capable of drawing its entire 2.8 million acre feet of water from the Colorado. Continuing the long Arizona tradition of poking a stick in the eye of California whenever it could, it has been sucking every drop out of the Colorado that it is entitled to. Although it does not need all of the water, and despite the fact that pumping the water out of the river and into central Arizona is costly, state officials are continuing to pull the water off the river and substituting it for surface water supplies or directly injecting it into groundwater aquifers.

States up and down the basin woke up to their long-feared nightmare as the powerful beast called California continued to drain more water out of the Colorado than it was entitled to, and continued to build its economy around that expected water supply. Would California acknowledge its limits and wean its way back to its rightful share?

The voice of the federal government, Secretary of the Interior Bruce Babbitt, entered the picture and warned California to produce a plan that would bring the state back within its 4.4-million-acre-foot entitlement. Facing a crackdown, the state parties explored a variety of means to make water needs fit within the stricture. In addition to finding water savings through infrastructure improvements, the biggest savings would be earned by trimming the profligate water use in the agricultural community and shifting some of the conserved water to the urban users on the coast.

Empirically, it looked easy. In addition to the huge differential of Imperial's water price of $15 to the cities' $300 or more, only a relatively modest amount of water, by Imperial Valley standards, was needed. If the Imperial Irrigation District, for example, could save 200,000 or 300,000 acre feet of water—approximately 5 percent to 10 percent of its water supply—that would satisfy the needs of urban users. And given the fact that the district had managed to service its farmers for many years by delivering 2.8 or 2.9 million acre feet—rather than today's 3.1 million acre feet—it looked like that type of savings could be obtained without any appreciable negative impact on the traditional needs of valley farmers.

Negotiations have not, however, proved to be easy in any sense of the word. Among other obstacles, the legal tools that were crafted a hundred years ago to guarantee water to best uses—farming and mining—have proved to be obdurate to today's more elastic needs. Even if Imperial Valley was interested in selling water to San Diego, the Coachella Water District is next in priority, and it believed that it had the legal right to the water first. Meanwhile, San Diego needed Los Angeles's help in transporting conserved water to San Diego. And the secretary of the interior, who held contracts with each of the agencies that included provisions that appeared to bar the transfer, had to negotiate new contracts that were mutually acceptable to all affected parties.

Months of negotiations ensued. Historic resentments flared as the lawyer-scriveners worked alongside the elected members of the water districts boards. Pressed by the secretary of the interior to get the deal done, and spurred by the bipartisan team of California's Governor Pete Wilson, first, and then Governor Gray Davis, the parties soldiered on. Lloyd Allen and Imperial seemed prepared to dedicate a relatively small percentage of its water to an urban transfer, so long as cities agreed to stop accusing Imperial of wasting water.

As the long process dragged on, environmental reviews came forward, revealing new challenges to the transaction. Because Imperial Valley would be conserving water, there would be less water flowing into the Salton Sea. And because the Salton Sea's longevity was tied to farm overflows, the transfer arguably would hasten the death of the sea. The environmental issues grew in importance, talk of the need to idle farmland increased, and the uneasy farmers' long-held concerns that they may not be in the Imperial Valley—Mr. Allen's constituents—questioned whether they were doing the right thing in selling water—their "birthright" and heritage—to the ungrateful city folks, became even more acute.

And so, despite the apparent inevitability to the water transfer, the negotiations have turned into a multiyear marathon. Along the way, the stakes have been raised even further as Secretary of the Interior Gale Norton has halted surplus flows of Colorado River water to California and sought to cut back the Imperial Irrigation District's water supply due to its alleged waste of some of it. A court challenge ensued, then feverish negotiations with the governor. More long meetings, more sweeteners into the pot, but still the final deal remains elusive.

The transfer of water to California's cities will come about. It has to. But the saga illustrates the profound change in water politics in today's America. Accommodation was the old way of resolving frictions in the water world—through a legal system that avoided fights by giving copious water rights to those who were there first; through a legislative system that produced expensive new dams and infrastructure to create new water supplies; and through a decision-making process that involved a tight group of insiders who rarely had to bother with pesky environmental issues, Native American water rights, or other "extraneous" distractions.

Accommodations still will need to be made to resolve water problems. Conflict increasingly will enter the process, as would-be dealmakers discover that the easy answers have been given long ago, that the stakes are higher than ever, and that win-win solutions are getting harder and harder to find.

Lloyd Allen (or his son) will do his deal. Just don't hold your breath. And watch for conflict-ridden, drawn-out poker games like Lloyd Allen's to spring up throughout our increasingly water-constrained nation.

PROSPECTS

Along with the multitude of issues associated with sufficient quantities of clean water, there are an equal number of theoretical solutions. The menu is broad: conservation, technology, innovation, creation of more of it, equitable access, changes in attitude, privatization, user pay, decentralization, and government intervention.

Even though there are many approaches to solving water issues, most agree that water needs to be treated differently than other resource problems, that water should be "above" the rules of the marketplace. Water is, for the most part, seen as a fundamental human need. Although there is general disgruntlement about how governments have managed water up to this point, most experts agree that they can never be completely disengaged from the distribution and regulation of water. The private sector is clearly becoming a growing player, though not the only player.

Perhaps the most important consideration for the future is a shift in attitude. The assumption that the water crisis will solve itself is flawed. An overconfidence in technology to find sufficient water to fuel the burgeoning economies that require more and more of it, regardless of the overall ecological context, is dangerous.

Acknowledging the entire ecological context is vital, for it recognizes the importance of the hydrologic cycle, the process that transforms salty water into fresh water through evaporation and then redistributes it. An important player in that cycle is the forest; it catches, holds, and recycles water in a miraculous, complex process. It distributes water in a timely manner, cleanses it of impurities, and releases it into the sky through transpiration. A forest can modify the temperature, even an entire climate. When a forest is cleared, soils harden, erode, and flood. Forests are clearly high on the list when considering the future of water. Acknowledging this is an important step as it implies a different relationship, a shift in attitude, with an important ecological feature: not one of management but of dependence.

This more holistic approach is beginning to emerge from some of the finest minds and organizations working in the field of water. This approach is opening the door for innovations to be developed from old technologies and solutions (i.e., dams, irrigation) as well as a serious reexamination of just how much is needed and for what.

Since agriculture continues to be the largest consumer of water worldwide—up to 80 percent in any given country—it is fortunate that some of the most innovative work is being done in this field. Irrigation has been severely criticized in recent years, some of it for good reason. However, the field of irrigation contains a huge potential for water-efficiency improvements. The gap is closing between the volume of water actually required by crops and the amount of irrigation poured onto them. Irrigation is being reinvented for the 21st century with innovative techniques such as furrow diking, land leveling, direct seeding, drip irrigation, and micro-sprinklers.

Drip irrigation uses plastic tubing on or under the soil surface. Very small holes deliver water directly to the plant roots in small quantities and under very low pressure. There is virtually no evaporation using this technique. At the moment, only one percent of irrigated fields use drip irrigation, so the potential for increased efficiency using this method alone is enormous. The costs have been prohibitively high but are dropping, making it a real possibility for small farmers and in developing countries; the Bedouin are now using drip irrigation on their oasis crops.

Although drip irrigation doesn't work with grain crops, low-pressure spraying does, using 30 percent less water than conventional spraying. Further efficiencies are realized by the timing of irrigation—applying small amounts of water just in time to alleviate severe moisture stress during the most sensitive stages of crop growth. In this way productivity can be increased even when the amount of water supplied is decreasing.

Inroads are also being made in the discovery of "new" water. Water is required for a variety of uses, but the quality needed varies too; not all of it has to be potable. Treated effluent is one of the more exciting potential sources for new water. Multiple-pipe distribution networks, once thought to be too expensive, are now seen as the device of choice for this new approach to delivering water. Using reclaimed wastewater to irrigate parks and golf courses and as a source for some agricultural uses solves a number of problems: pollution, water scarcity, and crop production. New water is also being found through water harvesting—the collection of rainwater.

Desalination is another emerging technology for creating fresh water. High costs have discouraged this practice in the past, but now the costs are dropping. This doesn't refer only to salt water, but to brackish groundwater and reclaimed municipal water as well.

The conservation approach is also gaining momentum; hundreds of proven water-efficiency measures address both short-term crises such as droughts and long-term shortages. Although water conservation measures usually require an investment up front, the time needed to pay back the investment is relatively short at around two years.

One example of conservation in urban North America is natural landscaping. By using native plants, very little, if any, supplemental watering is required. Indoors, the simple act of toilet flushing is the largest use of water in Western homes. This is an activity that may in fact not require water at all; new technology has produced an electronic composting toilet that is odorless, safe, and, unfortunately, still quite expensive.

A great way to motivate water conservation is a pricing structure that better reflects water's value. In some cases, this has resulted in unusual horse-trading among buyers and sellers of water; Los Angeles has invested in conservation improvements in nearby irrigation districts in exchange for the use of the water that has been saved. A situation that could have been competitive has become cooperative.

Removing water subsidies is another promising option. Many experts believed that this would mean rising food prices, but the results prove otherwise. Dropping subsidies in agriculture has resulted in a 33 percent drop in water use. Urban centers that have adopted full user-pay systems have found that consumption has dropped as much as 40 percent. And although many feared that removing water subsidies would hurt the poor most, it appears to affect the rich more because they are the greatest consumers of water. This approach has not been without its problems; some spectacular scandals have taken place, particularly with large French privatized water suppliers.

The underlying premise of paying the true cost of water is recognition of the ecological cost of maintaining our current rate of development and growth. Estimates of the full cost of nature's "services," including those performed by water, are in the tens of trillions of dollars per year. This begs another look at any assumption that endless growth is possible.

To further complicate the situation, climate change is looming as a force not easily reckoned with, at least not in the short term. The scientists who created the "Climate Change 2001" report believe that temperatures may rise by close to 6°C by the end of this century. The impact on glaciers alone is staggering; Kilimanjaro's ice cap has diminished by 75 percent since 1912, glaciers in the Canadian Rockies are shrinking, Venezuela has lost all but two of its glaciers, and the Gangotri Glacier, feeding the Ganges River, is receding at the rate of five meters a year. These important water-storage sources are disappearing at the same time that human demands are growing. The downstream impact is only now beginning to be understood.

We know that water is absolutely necessary for life. There is refocused attention on the world's most critical water needs, and the UN has set an explicit goal—to reduce by 50 percent the proportion of people who don't have access to safe drinking water by the year 2015. A new coalition is emerging: business, government, local communities, environmentalists, and the scientific community. There is no shortage of criticism and concern about some of these new partnerships, but one thing is clear: More stakeholders than ever before are at least at the table discussing the issues.

Is there the will to solve the world's water issues? Potential solutions abound. But whether one is a farmer, a scientist, an individual homeowner, or the owner of a pulp and paper mill, each must have the desire. Solving the problems is directly linked to our willingness to change our attitudes and our behaviors because fresh water, unlike other essential natural resources, is one that often—not always—has no substitute.

MOUNTAIN WATER:

LIFEBLOOD OF THE PRAIRIES

David Schindler

John Palliser, who explored the Canadian prairies in the mid-19th century, left behind journals from 1860 that have become famous for their documentation of extremely dry conditions. Even 150 years ago, he speculated that some areas would be "comparatively useless" for agriculture. These regions, which form the driest parts of Alberta and Saskatchewan, have since been termed "Palliser's Triangle."

Despite his dour predictions, settlers colonized the prairies during the ensuing several decades, and they eked out a living from the land. Ironically, recent studies using paleoecological indicators such as tree rings or algal fossils in lake muds have shown that this period of settlement was actually one of the wettest in the past several millennia. The period of Palliser's visit appears to be more typical of the two previous millennia. In any average century of the past 2,000 years, there have been three or four droughts. As a rule, at least one of those droughts exceeded ten years in length. Even the famous drought of the "dirty '30s" would have ranked as very minor in the context of the past two millennia.

Some of the prairie droughts were aggravated by warm conditions. The warmest period since the last glaciation was approximately 4,000 to 6,000 years ago, in a period called the mid-Holocene. There is disturbing evidence of serious water shortages on the prairies at the time. Lake Manitoba, the 12th largest lake in North America, was completely dry, as evidenced by grasses embedded in lake sediments of that age. Lake Winnipeg was nearly dry. Because the Saskatchewan River, which has always been by far the greatest source of water for Lake Winnipeg, originates in the Rockies, it's probable that mountain water sources were reduced as well.

Wetlands on the prairies were nearly nonexistent during the mid-Holocene. Many of these wetlands are intricately connected to the groundwater aquifers that are fed by mountain precipitation. Through all of these indicators, it's clear that in the past, extremely dry conditions have existed, even drier than at present. This was before man's demands and modifications to hydrological pathways and the atmosphere began, well before the first farmers arrived.

Most of the large Canadian prairie rivers originate in the snowpacks and glaciers of the Rocky Mountains, flow through the foothills, nourish the lowlands, and eventually empty into three oceans. The Columbia and Fraser Rivers flow to the Pacific. The Athabasca and Peace Rivers are the headwaters of the Mackenzie River, which flows to the Arctic Ocean. The Saskatchewan system flows from the ice fields to the Atlantic via Lake Winnipeg, the Nelson River, and Hudson's Bay.

The Saskatchewan River and its tributaries have made human habitation possible on the prairies, providing water for the agriculture and industry that attracted settlers in the late 19th and the 20th century. Today, they provide the water supplies for most of the large western prairie cities. The North Saskatchewan River originates in the mountains of west central Alberta, flowing northwest through Edmonton, Prince Albert, and smaller population centers. The southern branch originates in Banff National Park, where the Bow Glacier feeds the headwaters of the Bow River, which supplies water to Calgary. To the north, the Red Deer River supplies the city of the same name, and to the south the Oldman River supplies Lethbridge and Medicine Hat. Near the Saskatchewan border, the three tributaries join to form the South Saskatchewan, which provides Saskatoon with water before joining the North Saskatchewan. From there the river flows westward to Lake Winnipeg, where it has historically been the major source of water for that lake; it then exits via the Nelson River to Hudson's Bay. This represents an enormous geographical territory, most of it prairie, all sustained by rivers originating in the Rocky Mountains.

On the prairies, trees are abundant only in the riparian zones along rivers. These low-lying forested river valleys provided settlers with wood for the construction of buildings and for winter heating. Before roads were built, the rivers were also used as transportation corridors. It's not surprising that the larger prairie cities are located on these life-giving rivers.

Annual river flows are heavily dependent upon the annual snowpack in the Canadian Rockies, which can vary enormously from year to year. Snowfalls generally depend on the position of the jet stream, with dry conditions occurring when it is unusually far north and west. Much of the annual mountain snowpack melts in the period from April to June. In average or above average years, this spring freshet, or runoff, fills the reservoirs that have been constructed on these river systems, which then supply water and hydroelectric power to farmers and communities downstream.

In mid- and late summer, after the annual snowpacks have largely disappeared, prairie river flows become dependent on the melting of glaciers at the highest elevations of the Rockies. The annual combination of snowmelt in the spring and glacial melt in the summer has traditionally been sufficient to provide at least some water to the prairies throughout the entire year.

The groundwater of the prairies also originates in the Rockies. The elevation differences of 2,000 meters and more drive water through the subterranean aquifers that flow slowly eastward, providing groundwater and seepage to wetlands and lakes as far east as western Manitoba. This is a very slow process; it can take hundreds of years for water to travel that far, replenishing the subterranean aquifers hundreds of miles away. If we deplete the aquifers, recovery will be very slow. Life on the prairies is dependent on the well-being of those aquifers. Whether it's growing hay, watering city lawns, or maintaining natural ecosystems, the connection between prairie life and mountain water is a direct one.

For the past several years, the average annual snowpack in the Rockies has been unusually low. In addition, in southern regions of the prairies, periodic warm-weather winter melts have allowed much of the snowpack to seep away during the winter, when it is of little use to farmers and ranchers. Some optimistically regard the current situation as just another pesky prairie drought, which will end in a few years as all the others recorded by human history have done. However, recent studies indicate that 21st-century droughts may be different, because the effects of climate warming and human demand for water have added stresses that were not present in the past.

Drought will have increasingly severe consequences because the hydrological landscape has been significantly altered. Wetlands have been destroyed, rivers channelized, riparian zones destroyed, and surface water and groundwater removed for human use, including industry and agriculture. The climate of the western prairies is the warmest since the last glaciation period. Most scientists believe that much of this warming is the result of human release of greenhouse gases. Already, the temperature at various Alberta meteorological sites has increased by 1° C to 4° C in the past 50 to 100 years. The resulting increase in evaporation from land and water surfaces will certainly intensify drought conditions. Glaciers are melting more and more rapidly as the climate has warmed. Smaller glaciers have all but disappeared. The famous Athabasca Glacier of Jasper National Park, which is the origin of the boreal river of the same name, has retreated by 1.5 kilometers in 70 years, and is losing 16 million cubic meters of water per year more than it regains from winter snows.

To make matters worse, at the same time that water supplies are dwindling, human demands are increasing. Over three million people now live on the western prairies. They have brought with them more than 15 million head of livestock, all dependent on water. Seventy percent of licensed water withdrawals are used by prairie farmers for irrigating crops, and little of this water makes its way back to the rivers of its origin. But the demands aren't coming only from agriculture. Large quantities of water are pumped into deep wells to facilitate petroleum extraction; this water is permanently removed from the water cycle. These human stressors can only amplify the effects of natural droughts and climate warming, making water very scarce, and much more valuable.

Climatological history suggests that we are long overdue for a major drought, like those that lasted a decade or longer in centuries past. The recent four-year drought was already more intense than any in the 120 years or so that instrumental climate records on the prairies have been kept. It was even more intense than the famous drought of the 1930s. The evidence is everywhere and the impacts on rural communities have been serious. The impacts have cost billions of dollars in crops plowed under, closed businesses, decreased grain production, and insufficient feed for livestock. Many farmers have abandoned the land.

As a result of the past four dry years, most prairie wetlands are dry. Waterfowl breeding on the prairies is very low. Lake levels have declined by from one to over four meters. Some lakes, such as Muskiki Lake near Saskatoon in central Saskatchewan or Lake Maglore near Grand Prairie in northern Alberta, have gone completely dry. The community of Humboldt, Saskatchewan, has had to replace lost groundwater with a pipeline from the South Saskatchewan River, 193 kilometers away. In Alberta, the communities of Acme, Beiseker, Blackfals, Carbon, Hobbema, Irricana, Lacombe, and Ponoka have only a few short years remaining of their groundwater reserves, and they are proposing similar pipelines to the Saskatchewan River or its tributaries. These pipelines will cost hundreds of millions of dollars. Each will drain several million liters of water per day from the Saskatchewan River system if these towns and outlying farms continue to use water at current levels. Okotoks has already declared a complete moratorium on development as a result of water shortages. Linden's groundwater level decreased by 3.7 meters in a single year, 2001-02.

These are but a few of the prairie communities that are on the verge of severe water shortages. This scenario is repeated up and down the eastern slopes of the Rocky Mountains of North America.

Despite the scientific evidence that water supplies are precarious, population growth, livestock culture, industry, and wetland and riparian destruction continue to increase. There is no sign that federal or provincial governments are doing anything of substance to promote prudent water usage or watershed conservation.

Most of the recommendations of the 1987 Federal Water Policy still have not been implemented. Water quality is protected only by federal "guidelines" rather than enforceable standards, and provincial regulations are equally weak. Canada has diverted more water than any other nation in the world. About 70 percent of wetlands in southern Canada have been drained or filled. If our population and industry continue to grow and, at the same time, climate warming continues to melt the snowpacks and ice fields of the Rockies, we will face some hard choices about water use in the western prairies in the very near future.

Carbon dioxide already emitted is predicted to increase climate warming by another 1° to 2° in the near future. Data show that atmospheric CO_2 will double by the middle of the 21st century if we do not reduce our greenhouse gas emissions, which will cause even further modeling. Some climate models indicate that warming in the western prairies will be more rapid than the global average.

As climate warms, more frequent midwinter melts will probably allow snowpacks to increasingly seep away in January through March, when they are of little use to humans. In some areas of southern Alberta, spring snowmelt is predicted to supply only half as much water as it did in the late 20th century. In short, there are reasons to believe that the spring freshet from the Rockies that has nourished the western prairies—the sprawling ranches and rolling farmlands—will decline.

The prospect is even more dismal for the glacial melt that has supplied water to prairie rivers in midsummer and autumn. Glacier National Park in Montana is predicted to be glacier free by the mid-

21st century. The ice fields of Waterton, Banff, and Jasper are melting rapidly, and are sure to follow this pattern into oblivion.

The timing of the impending water shortage could not be worse for the industrial boom that is causing a population explosion in the province of Alberta. Calgary has grown by 20 percent in the past five years, and industrial demands are increasing. The effects of growing human demands combined with climate warming will bring a resounding halt to the "Alberta Advantage," as the economic boom of the 1990s is called by politicians, unless strong actions are taken on a number of fronts: conserve water, limit industries that require large amounts of water, and reduce emissions of greenhouse gases.

It's not only the prairies that depend on the mountains for their water. The "water towers" of the Rockies are also important to the western boreal landscape. The Peace, Athabasca, and Slave Rivers carry most of the water that flows through the boreal regions of Alberta.

Historically, these rivers have joined those of the prairies as important vectors for human exploration, commerce, and settlement. They were major transportation arteries for aboriginal people, who subsequently passed their knowledge on to the earliest explorers. Supplies and furs were transported between the Saskatchewan and Athabasca Rivers via the historic portage near Lac la Biche. Even in the late 19th century, the railroad ended in the northern Alberta city of Edmonton; goods were then transported by cart to Athabasca Landing, where riverboats and canoes distributed them all the way to the Beaufort Sea in the far north. Furs were brought south via the same route.

These rivers are as crucial today. Logging, petroleum, and mining industries supply thousands of people in boreal regions with a livelihood. These industries depend on mountain water for pulp and paper mills, oil sands extraction, and hydroelectric power. All of these industries are seriously jeopardized by declining flows from mountain rivers.

The Peace, largest of the rivers of the western Rockies, has current flows that are only about 60 percent of those in the early and mid-20th century. Human intervention—the construction of Bennett Dam—combined with lower snowfalls in the crucial headwater areas and climate warming are believed to have caused the declines.

This 60 percent decline has had disastrous consequences for the vast Peace-Athabasca Delta, the largest freshwater delta in western North America. The delta once served as an important breeding and staging area for migratory waterfowl. It also supported large populations of muskrats, moose, and fish that formed the basis for subsistence of a considerable aboriginal population. Before 1970, the delta was flooded an average of one year out of three. Since 1970, when the Bennett Dam was completed, the climate has warmed considerably and the delta has received only two major floods. Muskrats have all but vanished. Some of the "perched" lakes that required frequent floods from the Peace for refilling are now dry. There is no longer a thriving subsistence economy for aboriginal people in this area.

This situation is serious. Fresh water appears to be so plentiful that Canadians have become very cavalier in water use, ranking as the second most prolific water users in the world at

1,500 cubic meters each year. Water use by prairie residents is as profligate as anywhere else in the country. Yet the media continue to assure Canadians that they reside in a water-rich country. Only yesterday, prairie newspapers claimed "The Drought Is Over," as the result of unusual late spring snows in Alberta. I doubt this; drought will soon be back in the western prairies. Climate warming is already compromising mountain freshwater supplies that support ranchers, farmers, urban dwellers, the oil industry, mining, and entire communities. As I have mentioned, these effects are irreversible, because even if we take actions to curb greenhouse warming now, models predict that the climate will continue to warm for several decades. Once the glaciers have melted, they will not return until the next ice age. The best that we can do is to take rapid action to slow glacial melting by minimizing climate warming. This is done by reducing emissions of carbon dioxide and other greenhouse gases into the atmosphere.

Survival of the impacts of climate change on mountain water supplies to the western prairie regions will be aided by other conservation measures. We have to stop modifying riparian zones and wetlands, and they must be restored where possible, both in rural and urban areas. This will help to recharge aquifers and maintain stream flows. We can also make water reuse a greater priority. Instead of the wasteful use of high-purity water that we now practice, "gray" water that has drained down our sinks and showers can be used for flushing toilets and watering lawns and gardens. We can reduce industrial and agricultural water consumption by improved efficiency of application, reuse, or selection for industries that do not consume vast quantities of water. To ensure that our dwindling and precious water supplies are of the highest quality, we must reduce pollution from both nutrients and toxins. This requires improved treatment of sewage, storm drainage, and agricultural wastes as well as decreased use of fertilizers and pesticides. Our restoration of riparian and wetland areas is very important because they have the capacity to remove contaminants as well as act as "capacitors" in our network of freshwaters.

At present, little has been done by governments to protect fresh water. Federal and provincial budgets for freshwater research and monitoring, which were healthy 30 years ago, have been steadily reduced to very low levels. For example, Environment Canada spent 582 million dollars (Canadian) on science and technology funding in 1990. By 1999 the budget had decreased to 424 million. During the same period provincial spending on environmental research decreased by more than 50 percent. Neither of these figures is corrected for inflation. There have been further provincial cuts since these figures were released.

Perhaps the most difficult task is to reconsider just how much growth of human population and industry is desirable. Most residents of the prairies choose to live there because they value empty spaces, unimpaired ecosystems, and a sense of freedom.

We know that in the past, shortage of fresh water has limited the advancement of human civilization in other parts of the world. Desertification of previously fertile areas has not been uncommon; people moved on, abandoning the landscape that could no longer sustain them, looking for another promised land. It can happen on the Canadian prairies, too, if we continue to squander this most precious of natural resources. Where will these farmers go, and how long before the next promised land has also run dry because we didn't learn to manage our water more carefully?

A CHILD'S REMINDER

David Suzuki with Amanda McConnell

f air is the spirit that animates all living things, water gives them body and substance. Water was absolutely necessary for life as we know it to have evolved. Life originated in the oceans, and the salty taste of our blood reminds us of our marine evolutionary birth. But humans, like many other animals and plants, cannot live on salt water. Our lives are made possible by the hydrologic cycle, the miraculous process whereby salty water is transformed into fresh water by evaporation and is redistributed around the planet.

A forest is an intricate device for catching, holding, using, and recycling water. That tangle of tree roots snaking across the forest floor absorbs water while holding the soil so effectively that creeks don't flood and the water flowing in them is clean and clear after many days of rain. Held in the soil, in roots and trunks and branches, the water is slowly meted out over days and weeks, and any excess is returned to the air. Millions of tons of water in tropical rain forests are lifted from the soil back into the sky by transpiration. Large areas of forest create their own local weather, raining on themselves and remaining moist during dry spells. At the same time, they modify the climate of the entire region and beyond. When large tracts of tropical rain forest are removed, the barren soil hardens, causing rain to evaporate or run off rapidly.

The hydrologic cycle allows the nonpotable water of the oceans to fall from the skies as sweet water and sustain life on the land. Even though only a minute quantity of potable water—2.54 percent of all water on Earth—is readily accessible to land organisms through rivers, lakes, and groundwater, the hydrologic system draws fresh water from the oceans and land and returns it as rain and snow. Each year, over 113,000 billion cubic meters of water fall to Earth, enough to cover all the continents to a depth of 80 centimeters. Two-thirds of this amount evaporates back into the atmosphere; surface and subsurface waters are replenished by the rest. That water is not evenly distributed, of course; some regions get a great deal of water and others do not get much at all, depending on climate, latitude, elevation, and weather patterns. The amount of water determines the nature and abundance of vegetation in each region. The vast continent of Australia, for example, is often referred to as "underpopulated"; in fact, it is too poor in water in relation to its land base to support a larger human population. In contrast to the great rivers meandering through the heart of North America—the Mississippi, the Columbia, the Mackenzie—an enormous desert occupies the center of Australia.

Life is opportunistic, taking advantage of niches through mutation and new combinations of genes. Plants and animals have evolved to exploit both marine and freshwater environments. The oceans are filled with plants—immense kelp forests and massive blooms of phytoplankton that are the base of the marine food chain. The abundance of forms that cooperate to make the coral reef communities, the forests of mangroves lining the ocean beaches, and the gatherings of creatures in estuaries all attest to the power of evolution to hone organisms for diverse habitats. On land, plants and animals alike have found strategies to flourish where water is rare. Species are found in the ice of polar sheets, on arid mountaintops, and in the dry heart of the desert. Anadromous fishes such as eels and salmon have evolved life cycles that exploit both marine and freshwater environments, and numerous species inhabit both water and air or water and land at different stages of their life cycles. But no species has evolved to do without water, and no species has been as imaginative and as demanding in its use of water as human beings.

We are water. Our cells are inflated by water, our metabolic reactions mediated in aqueous solution. Water is created in the metabolism of life; we absorb it from solid food and from any liquid we imbibe. Every day each of us requires about 2.5 liters of water to compensate for what is lost from our bodies to maintain a constant internal balance, but that amount can represent a small fraction of the water that we use for other reasons or that is used on our behalf in farming or industry. But not all people have equal access to the water supply. A person in an industrialized country uses between 350 and 2,000 liters of water daily, whereas a person living in rural Kenya, for example, may use two to five liters. Many water-rich countries, such as Canada, use water as if it were limitless, often meeting food, energy, and material needs through the copious use of water, whether they know it or not. On any North American dinner table, the vegetables may have been produced by irrigation, hydroelectric power may have cooked them, and the dish they're served in may have taken liters of water to manufacture. Industry uses water on our behalf in a multitude of ways—as the medium wherein chemicals are mixed and react or simply to carry material such as wood fibers in pulp or for washing away excess material.

When humans acknowledge dependence on the same biophysical factors that support all other life-forms, believing that we have the responsibility for "managing" all of it becomes a terrible burden. But if we look at all of life together, we may recognize that we are not the "managers." There is wisdom enough for self-management in the web of living creatures that has survived for more than 3.6 billion years. Instead of trying, and failing, to manage the life-support systems of the planet, we can manage the effect we have on those systems. To that end, there are many things that each of us can do.

We must think deeply about some of our most widely held assumptions, since many underlie the destructive path we're on. It is widely believed that intellect has lifted human beings out of the natural world into a human-created environment. Yet our absolute need for air, water, soil, energy, and biodiversity belies that assumption.

Many believe that science and technology provide the understanding and tools to manage nature and to find solutions to problems that science and technology have helped to create. Technology does provide powerful instruments for very straightforward activities. But science can fragment the way we see the world, so we have no context within which to see what impact our activities and technological applications have.

We assume that even though we are just one of perhaps 30 million species, the entire planet is ours for the taking. We assume that we can manage our natural resources through the bureaucratic subdivisions of government and industry. We assume that we can do environmental assessments and cost/benefit analyses to minimize the impact of what we do. All of these assumptions fail to stand up to critical analysis that includes the full ecological cost of our impact.

Some believe that a clean environment is only affordable when the economy is strong, but in fact we need to reflect on how we can meet our fundamental needs while simultaneously making a living. To do so means that our economy has to be connected to the world of the biosphere. Estimates of the annual cost of "services" performed by nature, such as cleansing air and water, pollinating plants, inhibiting erosion and flooding, building topsoil and so on, reach the tens of trillions of dollars. Yet conventional economics ignores these services as "externalities." A true Earth economy would take these services into account. The notion that growth is the definition of progress is suicidal; as ecologist Paul Ehrlich has noted, endless growth in a finite world is the creed of the cancer cell.

Our attempts to ward off the negative consequences of our activities must be made at the "top of the pipe," not at the end. That is, we must try to avoid problems such as pollution or climate change by preventing the cause of the problem rather than trying to solve the problem after it exists. In the long run, sustainable living demands a fundamental shift in values, which must then be translated into action. We must get involved. Volunteer your services if possible. In the process, one learns and becomes committed.

The place to begin is at home: Work to make your home as ecologically benign as possible. Of the three R's—reduce, reuse, recycle—reducing is by far the most important precept. Begin by questioning the notion that throwaway items are acceptable. Make "disposable" an obscene word and favor the reusable over the recyclable.

Industries that are designing means of production can follow the example of nature in which one species' waste is another's opportunity. A plant that uses energy from the sun to grow and reproduce may also nourish a host of parasites and herbivores, and upon dying feed still other life-forms while returning organic material to the soil to nurture future generations of plants. Material is used, transformed, and used again in a never-ending cycle. We can change our thinking from the linearity of extracting, processing, manufacturing, selling, using, and discarding into the circularity of natural cycles.

The shift in thinking must be informed by the reality of the global ecological situation. You needn't be confused about which expert to believe; talk to elders around you, people who have lived in your part of the world for the past 70 or 80 years. Ask them what they remember about the air, about other species, about the water, about neighborhoods and communities. Our elders tell us of the immense changes that have occurred in the span of a single human life; project the rate of change they have experienced into the future to get an idea of what might be left in the coming decades. Is this progress? Is this way of life sustainable? Consider the problems that we are leaving as a legacy for our children and grandchildren. What will the quality of their air, water, and soil be like? What kind of food will they eat? How much wilderness will be left for them to enjoy?

My family's ten-day visit to the village of Aucre in the Amazon rain forest in Brazil took place in 1989, when my daughters Severn and Sarika were nine and five years old, respectively. As we flew away from the village, we could see the encroachment of gold miners who were polluting the rivers and destroying the riverbanks, and farmers burning the forest in a desperate search for land on which to grow food. Severn became alarmed about the future of her newfound friends in Aucre, and upon returning to Vancouver, she started a club called ECO (Environmental Children's Organization). Five 10-year-old girls began to speak out about the beauty of tropical forests; the animals, plants, and people who inhabit them; and the need to protect them. Over time, the girls were invited to visit classes and give talks, gaining some local notoriety.

Severn told me that she wanted to take ECO to the Earth Summit in Rio de Janeiro in June 1992. This conference would bring together the largest gathering of heads of state in history.

"I think all those grown-ups will be talking about our future," Severn said, "and they need us there to act as their conscience." I vigorously protested, pointing out that it would be expensive, that Rio was polluted and dangerous, and besides, it was unlikely that children would be heard. I promptly forgot about the conversation. Yet two months later, Severn proudly displayed a check made out to ECO for a thousand dollars from an American philanthropist to whom she had spoken about her dream.

At the Earth Summit, ECO registered as a nongovernmental organization and rented a booth at the Global Forum along with hundreds of other groups. They set up a display of pictures and posters, handed out their newspapers and brochures about ECO, and talked to many people. Soon reporters and television cameras appeared to interview these five girls from Canada. The Canadian Environment Minister, Jean Charest, made an appearance with cameras in tow. Eventually William Grant, the U.S. head of UNICEF, heard the girls speak and persuaded Maurice Strong, the organizer of the Earth Summit, to invite Severn to address a plenary session.

Severn was 12 years old. She wrote her speech, with input from her fellow ECO members, and rehearsed it over and over during the taxi ride to Rio Centro, the site of the conference. She was the last to speak. Some of what she said was this:

> I'm only a child and I don't have all the solutions, but I
> want you to realize neither do you. You don't know how
> to fix the holes in the ozone layer. You don't know how
> to bring the salmon back up a dead stream. You don't

know how to bring back an animal now extinct. And you can't bring back a forest where there is now a desert. If you don't know how to fix it, please stop breaking it.…

In my country, we make so much waste; we buy and throw away, buy and throw away. Yet northern countries will not share with the needy. Even when we have more than enough, we are afraid to lose some of our wealth, afraid to let go.…

You teach us how to behave in the world. You teach us not to fight with others; to work things out; to respect others; to clean up our mess; not to hurt other creatures; to share, not be greedy. Then why do you go out and do the things you tell us not to do?…

My dad always says, "You are what you do, not what you say," Well, what you do makes me cry at night. You grown-ups say you love us. I challenge you. Please, make your actions reflect your words.

The Earth Summit in Rio was attended by heads of state, nongovernmental organizations, scientists, educators, and environmental advocates. They agreed that the time for action was immediate. But it was the heartfelt words of a child that sent the challenge back to the decision-makers, and to the world, to convert words into action. Whether we are ten years old or fifty, we have an obligation to ourselves, to the Earth, to the children of this Earth, to recognize this sanctity, to do what we can to preserve this sacred liquid and influence all whom we can to do likewise. There may be no other time in history where our actions can make such a difference.

A SOFT PATH:

CONSERVATION, EFFICIENCY,

AND EASING CONFLICTS OVER WATER

Peter H. Gleick

The greatest water problems facing the world are not the result of inadequate infrastructure, but inefficient water use, inappropriate allocations, water pollution, and ecological destruction. And even in regions facing shortages, increasing supplies is the most expensive, slowest, and most environmentally damaging solution. Billions of people still lack safe drinking water and adequate sanitation services that were available to most citizens of ancient Rome. Millions die every year from preventable water-related diseases, and hundreds of millions more suffer from debilitating illnesses. Controversy is raging over the proper role of expensive dams and infrastructure, private corporations, and local communities in managing water. Municipalities are faced with billions of dollars of infrastructure needs and growing disputes over the role of public and private water management. Arguments in the western U.S. are growing over allocations of shared rivers, as are tensions between cities and farmers over water rights, such as in the Klamath Basin. The U.S. and Mexico have unresolved disagreements over border water resources, and our Canadian neighbors are concerned about proposals to divert Great Lakes or Canadian water for U.S. use.

For all the growing calls to address these problems, there is still little consensus about the best ways to move forward, hindering effective progress. A question being debated these days in the halls of Congress and by American intelligence agencies is whether water will become the oil of the 21st century. The question really contains two parts. Are we going to permit water to become a commodity like oil, to be overpumped, underpriced, and used wastefully, leading to water wars, international conflict and competition, and environmental destruction? And second, can we avoid the problems that have resulted from our dependence on oil by planning to ensure that water is used efficiently and allocated properly, through national policies and international cooperation, and that the environment is protected from damage caused by its extraction?

Amid the deep and justifiable gloom about the world's water crisis, it is worth calling attention to some glimmers of hope. Political cooperation over water is continuing in places with serious ongoing political disputes, like Israel and Jordan, and South Asia. Attention to meeting basic human needs in South Africa has helped millions receive water services previously unavailable. And growing efforts to reduce waste and increase efficient use are relieving tensions over water shortages. Since 1990, water use in southern California has dropped by 16 percent, even as the population has increased by nearly the same figure. In Seattle, total water use has remained constant since 1975, even as population has increased by 30 percent.[1] In Boston, water use has dropped by a full 30 percent since the late 1980s. In the past 20 years, per capita water use in the United States has declined a full 20 percent, even as population growth and economic growth have continued.

What is happening here? What these figures show is real progress toward efficiency—finding ways to stretch each drop of water further. They show a departure from the most worrying global trends, in which water use has increased even more quickly than population growth, and has increased most rapidly where economies are growing the most quickly. In the United States, as in most parts of the world, the fastest, cheapest, and most environmentally acceptable way to address water conflicts will in most cases not be an increase in supply, but improvements in efficiency to reduce waste and increase water supply reliability. Realizing these savings will be faster, cheaper, and more politically acceptable than any new supply option proposed, including new dams, desalination plants, or long-distance aqueducts.

To understand the choices ahead, it is important first to look back. The focus of water planners and managers in the 20th century was in finding ways to increase water supplies in every region of the country. This approach brought enormous benefits, including flood protection, clean water supplies, widespread irrigation and hydropower, and improved human health. Indeed, new water facilities must still be built in the future, especially in places where the basic infrastructure for water supply and sanitation is still inadequate. And more money must be spent on operating and maintaining the systems already built.

But that path also has had high and frequently unrecognized costs. It has often led to ecologically damaging, socially intrusive, and capital-intensive projects that failed to deliver promised benefits. This cannot be our approach in the 21st century. The use of water must be seen not as an end in itself, but as a means to an end.

At the most basic level, two paths lie before us. One, a "hard path," relies almost exclusively on centralized infrastructure to capture, treat, and deliver water in order to expand the available supply. The other, the "soft path," aims to improve the efficient and wise use of water through investments in decentralized facilities, efficient technologies and policies, smart application of economics, and community management and planning.[2] The soft path seeks to improve the overall productivity of water use rather than to find endless sources of new supply. It focuses on the idea of delivering water services matched to the needs of end users rather than just delivering water, and it works with users at appropriate scales.[3]

Simply put, a soft path for water emphasizes improving the productive use of the water that we already capture, clean, and use. It includes the concepts of water-use productivity, rational application of technology and economics, and decision-making at the right scale for the job. This approach must be contrasted to the unshakable belief that still exists among most water policymakers that large, centralized water systems are the only way to meet unrelenting growth in demand, and that such demand is an inevitable outcome of growth in population and gross domestic product.

Until recently it has generally been assumed that rates of water use and economic growth, like water use and population, increased hand in hand. But recent trends in the United States and other parts of the world have begun to belie that notion. Between 1900 and the mid-1990s, the U.S. gross domestic product increased 20-fold. Total water withdrawals increased more than ten times between 1900 and 1980, but then began to decline, and by 1995 they had dropped approximately 10 percent from their peak, even as economic growth continued to surge. A graph of the two trends would show lines moving in parallel and then a sharp fork in the road, as water use veered downward.

Even some developing nations are experiencing an uncoupling of economic growth and water use, although data on water use are infrequently and imperfectly collected. In China, estimates suggest, water use has continued to rise every year, but not nearly as rapidly as the rate of economic growth, which began to skyrocket in the mid-1980s.

Two factors are driving this uncoupling, both of them the products of technological innovation and water scarcity. The first is broad improvement in the productive use of water, meaning that with improvements in the ability to produce goods and services there is less demand for water. The second factor is a shift away from water-intensive industries. The mix of goods and services desired is changing over time in a direction that decreases water needs per unit output, and even total water needs.

In the past 20 years many economies have also begun to shift production away from water-intensive uses. Industries such as steel production, chemicals manufacture, and mining are becoming a less important part of overall economic activity, while industries that consume less water, such as service industries, telecommunications, and computing, have been assuming a larger role in the economy. The result has been a further divergence between economic production and water use. In the early 1970s, Hong Kong was producing around $500 (Hong Kong) for every cubic meter of water used; by 2000, its economic productivity of water had increased to nearly $1,000 (Hong Kong) per cubic meter.[4] Similarly, California's economic productivity of water has doubled from around $8 per cubic meters in the mid-1970s to over $16 per cubic meter in the late 1990s.[5]

Water-use efficiency can be improved through technological innovations, new policies, and simple improvements in operations and production. In the 1930s and 1940s, for example, steel production typically consumed as much as 200 to 300 tons of water per ton of steel. By the mid-1980s, overall water consumption to produce steel had declined to between 20 and 30 tons of water. Today, the most efficient plants consume only three to four tons of water per ton of steel.[6] Part of this improvement comes from the adoption of modern manufacturing techniques; part comes from efforts to reduce wastewater discharges to meet water-quality standards. The net result is an enormous increase in the overall water-use productivity in steel production.

Comparable improvements can be found in every economic sector. In the United States, the standard for commercial and residential toilets has been reduced from six gallons per flush to 1.6 gallons per flush—a 75 percent reduction—and commercially available toilets from Japan and Australia use even less than this. Washing machines are becoming far more water and energy efficient, further reducing overall residential water use. Simply by providing incentives for people to buy modern toilets and washing machines, and by retrofitting outdoor landscapes, the city of Albuquerque reduced per capita water use by 30 percent between 1989 and 2001.[7] In New York City, smart conservation produced a 25 percent dip in water use between 1979 and 2001, a savings of some 375 million gallons a day, as well as billions of dollars in avoided expenditures for new supply and treatment plants.[8]

Recent research suggests ample opportunity for further improvements. In California, for example, additional reductions of at least 40 percent in commercial and industrial water use are possible with existing technologies, studies by the Pacific Institute show. Even greater savings are possible in the residential sector and in agriculture, where drip irrigation and precision sprinkler systems can both boost crop yields and reduce water demands, saving water and money for farmers.

The agricultural sector currently accounts for more than two-thirds of all human water withdrawals; therefore, improving agricultural water-use productivity can help alleviate the rising concerns about food production for growing populations. Agricultural water-use efficiency can be vastly improved by changes in irrigation technology, including soil-moisture monitors, proper scheduling, laser leveling, and precision irrigation systems. These approaches not only cut down on water but could greatly increase productivity for many crop types. Recent experience with laser leveling in Arizona, which permitted more uniform and careful application of water, found that water use on wheat, alfalfa, and cotton fields declined between 20 percent and 32 percent and yields increased 12 percent to 22 percent.[9] A similar approach in the Tadla region of Morocco reduced water use by 20 percent and increased cereal crop yields by 30 percent.[10]

Shifting from conventional surface irrigation to drip in India increased overall water productivity (crop yield per unit water supplied) by between 45 percent and 255 percent on crops as diverse as bananas, cotton, sugarcane, and sweet potatoes.[11] In Jordan, drip irrigation combined with soil-moisture sensors increased cucumber and tomato crop yields 15 percent to 20 percent while reducing water use 20 percent to 50 percent—an overall increase in water-use efficiency of 44 percent to 140 percent.[12] Despite these reported improvements, however, only limited efforts to apply precision irrigation have been made. Worldwide, the area under micro-irrigation is estimated to be only about one percent of total irrigated land.[13] In general, planting less water-intensive, higher-valued crops will both improve water productivity and generate more income even without changing irrigation techniques. Such a shift has been quietly under way for two decades in California.[14] In the mid-1990s, nearly 60 percent of all water used by agriculture was used to grow rice, cotton, alfalfa, and irrigated pasture, yet these four crops produced less than 20 percent of total agricultural revenue. Switching even part of the acreage planted in these crops to less water-intensive, higher value crops resulted in considerable improvements in water-use efficiency.

Capturing these savings is not always easy, even when there are clear savings in money and water. Inappropriate subsidies often hide the benefits of conservation. New technology may be unfamiliar to water users. And traditional practices are sometimes difficult to overcome. There are other challenges, too. These include overhauling unfair pricing structures that encourage wasteful use of water, investing in water-wise technology, recycling and reusing water for the right purposes, and educating people about the potential for using water wisely and the benefits of doing so.

In many cases, solving these problems requires farsighted state and local action. But national leadership is also needed. Unfortunately, in the United States and most other countries, inadequate attention is being given to national water issues, and what efforts are being made are often contradictory or counterproductive. Responsibility for water is spread out over many federal agencies and departments, operating with no overall coordination. What is too often lost is the salient point that water conservation and efficiency do not just make sense; they make more sense than any other alternative available to us.

This is not the first time, after all, that major international efforts have targeted water-supply and sanitation needs. Beginning in the late 1970s, efforts were made to expand access to water-supply and sanitation services in the developing countries, but with only modest success. By 2000, despite massive investment from the World Bank, international aid organizations, and individual governments, an estimated 2.4 billion people still lacked adequate sanitation services—more than lived on the entire planet in 1940.[15] During this same period, many industrialized nations achieved modest improvements in water quality. But on a global scale, these have been overshadowed by the destruction of the Aral Sea, the shrinkage of Lake Chad in Africa, the drying up of the deltas of many of the world's major rivers, the loss of growing numbers of fish species, and the depletion of groundwater aquifers worldwide.

This deplorable state of affairs is the result of many past mistakes. Weak governments have remained unwilling or unable to devote the time or expertise to building or operating water systems. Ecosystems are ignored in water planning. Limited capital or competition for that money for other needs may inhibit spending for infrastructure improvements. International development efforts have been misdirected to massive water systems that fail to provide their expected benefits, or provide them to the wrong people. Rapid population growth in urban areas in particular is outstripping the ability of local governments to expand basic services. And inappropriate water policies or technologies often result in vast quantities of water being lost or used inefficiently.

Many components must be put together to forge a soft water path. But a critical first step is to evaluate how water is used and to rethink our needs and wants. The impediments to meeting our needs must also be identified, and tools developed to reduce those impediments. Finally, government agencies, communities, or water suppliers must implement comprehensive, integrated economic, educational, and regulatory policies that remove the barriers and move toward sustainable management and use of water.

There are several basic characteristics of a soft water path. First, human and ecosystem water needs must be the top priority, before other needs are met. Second, governments, communities, and private companies should work to meet water-related needs or services rather than to merely supply water. Third, the quality of water provided should more effectively match the quality of water required for any given purpose. Fourth, more extensive investments should be made in decentralized solutions, which are often less capital intensive and more user friendly. Fifth, water providers must work directly with community groups and water users to manage supplies, and especially water use, more effectively. And finally, appropriate economic tools are necessary to take account of a wider variety of costs and benefits of water supply and use than traditionally acknowledged.

Whether water-efficient technologies will become socially acceptable as they become economically competitive is an important question. Soft-path planners believe that farmers want to grow crops rather than use water, and will implement water-conserving technologies that make economic and social sense. A basic goal of the soft path is identifying the difference between needs and wants. Soft-path planners believe that most people want human wastes managed in a convenient, cost-effective, hygienic way, and that they will accept alternatives that use little or no water if these criteria are met.

The soft path is not easy to follow. It requires a change in concepts and beliefs. It requires institutional changes, new management tools and skills, and a greater reliance on actions by many individual water users rather than a small number of engineers. It requires some combination of regulations, economic incentives, new technologies, and retraining of water managers and the public. It is increasingly apparent, however, that continuing on the hard path may prove even more problematic. A new way of thinking about our scarce water resources is long past due. We know where the hard path leads—to a diminished natural world, concentrated decision-making, and higher economic costs. A more productive use of water, with open decision-making and acceptance of the ecological values of water, offers the promise of a brighter future.

ALCHEMY OR SALVATION?

DESALTING THE SEA

Douglas Jehl

San Diego gets very little rain, but it is home to 2.7 million people, and it is growing fast. It owes its beauty to the Pacific Ocean but its survival to its neighbors within the state and outside it, who provide 86 percent of its fresh water, most of it from the Colorado River. But now the county is getting ready to turn to the sea in a much bigger way, seizing on the ocean as "the world's largest reservoir." By 2007, if all goes as planned, the water utility will begin producing desalted seawater at a rate of 50 million gallons of fresh water a day, at a $270 million desalination plant that will become the hemisphere's largest. That will supply about 8 percent of the county's water needs, a leap forward toward a future in which some believe American and even worldwide water needs will be sustained by the oceans in ever greater measure.

As recently as 1993, San Diego had rejected desalination as too expensive. But with prices dropping fast, it is not the only place where seawater is winning converts. In Tampa, Florida, what is now the hemisphere's largest seawater desalination plant opened in March 2003. Its costs of producing fresh water from the ocean are lower than any other in the world, and along with San Diego, more than a dozen other communities in Florida, Texas, and California are hoping to follow suit. For the first time, seawater desalination efforts are winning funding from the state and federal governments; in New Mexico a national laboratory is searching for even more effective ways to make the sea drinkable. Over the next 10 to 15 years the Metropolitan Water District of Southern California, one of the largest in the country with 19 million customers, has set a goal of producing 150,000 acre feet of desalted seawater a year—enough for 300,000 households, or 1.2 million users, which is about 7 percent of its customers' needs. "Desalination is no longer on the lunatic fringe," said Barry Nelson, an expert at the Natural Resources Defense Council, an environmental group. "It has entered the mainstream."

Will Tampa and San Diego really set the mold? Can seawater desalination mean salvation from water woes? Or is it instead akin to alchemy, with more glittering potential than practical applicability, except in places where desperation and bad planning have left no other choice? Might more mundane solutions—like using more water again and again instead of trying to manufacture new supplies—be more cost-effective and prudent?

To weigh those prospects requires some thinking about the past and present. Certainly, the need for more fresh water has become acute. In supplying regions closest to the coast where energy costs are low, seawater can compete with other options. But so can solutions that reuse existing fresh water instead of manufacturing it, and those less glamorous approaches may be the most promising.

Consider, for example, the discomfiting picture painted by Steve Malloch of the Western Water Alliance, a coalition of conservationists, water users, and state officials. "In years of average precipitation," he writes in "The Western Way of Water," a June 2003 report, "water supplies in most of the West are already more than fully used. We get by because the West's major lakes and reservoirs help store some of the water from year to year, allowing wet years to help meet the needs of normal and dry years." That is an undeniably fragile architecture; when wet years become fewer or more widely spaced, as during the recent drought (or possibly the impact of global climate change), the whole system faces collapse. But to what extent is seawater the solution?

One place to start is southern California, where planners have had to confront more directly than in any other state the prospect that water supplies might not be sufficient to sustain its people. Like San Diego, California and southern California in particular has become a victim of its success, incapable without outside help of sustaining even a tiny fraction of its current population. As it tries to expand its supplies, from a base that comes primarily from northern California and from the Colorado River, it is only natural that the Metropolitan Water District is turning to the ocean.

But it is also worth keeping in mind that water is not necessarily consumed in the way that, say, food or electricity is consumed. Often what is pumped from an aquifer or siphoned from a stream ends up back in the same system, having passed through showers, washing machines and toilets, drains and sewers. The use of so-called gray water for watering or even drinking has become increasingly common, and it offers water managers another option for creating new water. In future plans, reused water will play an even larger role than seawater even in southern California, where projects that the big water district helped to fund in 2002 produced 75,000 acre feet of water. (An acre foot of water, the industry standard, is about 326,000 gallons, or the amount that two urban households consume in a year.) Combined with the 126,000 acre feet in reused water produced by its members without the district's financial assistance, the total of about 200,000 acre feet right now is more than the district hopes to produce from desalination a decade or more from now. The U.S. Bureau of Reclamation has identified another 34 projects that it says can yield more than 450,000 additional acre feet in the next few decades. That represents a real water source, not just a novelty; by using gray water for outdoor watering or collecting runoff, for example, water managers can add to supplies and minimize the need to seek out new sources.

The major exception is water used on crops, most of which disappears through evaporation and by passing through the roots. In California, for example, according to statistics assembled by the U.S. Geological Survey, agriculture accounts for 64 percent of water withdrawals but 93 percent of the water consumed. That means water shifted away from farms could have a disproportionate impact, because it would free up water that now is used only once but could be used again and again in efficient municipal and industrial systems.

Indeed, in southern California, the water district has made a major effort to buy up water from farms, particularly in the Imperial Valley, whose disproportionately huge title to most of the state's allotment of Colorado River water has long rankled the coastal cities. But the district has also concluded that they should at the same time try to tap the sea. The fact that Tampa, not San Diego, was the first large American city to turn to desalination offers a hint to the option's appeal.

Unlike southern California, central Florida is a region of abundant rain, with some 30 inches of precipitation a year. Tampa had acted for years as if its water sources were limitless, enough to serve a population whose explosion showed no signs of slowing down. As with most of Florida, nearly all Tampa's fresh water comes from underground, which made the illusion easier to sustain. But by the mid-1990s, groundwater pumping had begun to take an undeniable toll that could be measured in sinkholes, dying trees, and saltwater intrusion into freshwater aquifers. Under pressure from the courts, the Southwest Florida Water Management District promised to cut back on its pumping and shift away from what was proving an unsustainable course. Yet rivers, creeks, and reservoirs offered no real alternative. Although the sea is a source of last resort for drinking water, Tampa has embraced it. Since March 2003, the plant in Tampa has been sucking about 44 million gallons of seawater a day from the Gulf of Mexico, to produce about 25 million gallons of fresh water— about 10 percent of the water used by Tampa's nearly two million people.

Still, the Tampa plant needed several years to win approval from state regulators, caused by opposition that is a reminder of the misgivings still facing such projects. Even the most advanced desalination systems, like the one in Tampa, require about 1.8 gallons of seawater to produce a gallon of fresh water, leaving a briny by-product that must be disposed of. One concern has been that the release of briny water, twice as salty as the sea, could have a harmful effect on the underwater ecology. In Tampa, critics said they feared that desalination would result in a saltier Tampa Bay, with possible harm to water life, including some fish and perhaps the manatee, an endangered marine mammal. But several studies have suggested that the concerns are misguided. A study commissioned by Tampa Bay Water found no reasonable risk that salinity in the bay would build up over time. The research found that the estuary into which the outflows would be pumped already flushes naturally, and it pointed out that native species of fish and sea grass are already accustomed to salinity variations. But some independent experts have been more skeptical. Although the water discharged back into the bay is to be diluted with ordinary seawater, at a ratio of 70:1, the effects are being closely monitored, and indication of harm will almost certainly prompt a legal challenge.

Aesthetic concerns also posed an obstacle. Unlike a reservoir or a groundwater pump, a desalination plant is neither attractive nor easily hidden, and its neighbors, who organized themselves into groups with names like Save the Bay, were united in trying to keep a desalination plant out of their backyards. Only through an unusual process, in which a regional coalition had the power to override objections from the county that is home to the desalination plant, was the plant able to win political approval.

But the most important obstacle was financial. To promote desalination as an alternative to the groundwater pumping, the regional water authority put up 85 million dollars of $110 million in construction costs. But a private consortium that was to have owned and operated the plant found itself unable to win the financing it needed, and the water utility had to buy the project itself so that it could go forward. Production costs have turned out to be much lower than the $4 to $6 a gallon that was initially projected, and the cost of about $2.49 per 1,000 gallons remains the lowest of any desalination plant now in operation or planned. Because of the subsidy from the water district, the wholesale cost will be even lower, about $1.88 per 1,000 gallons.

That is less than any other seawater desalination plant now operating, in part because Tampa Bay, with its numerous freshwater inflows, is less salty than most oceans. Still, compared with more conventional methods of acquiring water, the costs are staggeringly high. They are nearly double the one-dollar-per-1,000-gallon cost of the groundwater on which Tampa had previously relied. Seawater desalination is not the only new source of water on which Tampa is relying, and all are expensive. They are expected to gradually drive up the wholesale water rate to between $2.34 and $2.91 per thousand gallons, up from $1.75 in 2003, a cost that will be passed on to customers.

Until Tampa took the plunge, only two American cities had invested in full-fledged seawater desalination plants—Key West, Florida, in the early 1980s, and Santa Barbara, California, a decade later. Both of those cities shut down their operations soon after they began, having lined up cheaper alternatives; their plants are now maintained to provide emergency backup. "It's still cheaper for us to pump fresh water 130 miles down here from the mainland than to make it from sea water," Jim Reynolds, deputy executive director of the Florida Keys Aqueduct Authority, told the *New York Times*. Those experiences should be interpreted as reasons for caution; desalination is not necessarily for everyone.

The largest seawater desalination plants in the world, and by far the heaviest concentration, are located in Saudi Arabia, Kuwait, and other countries on the arid Arabian Peninsula, whose supplies of fresh water are so scarce that desalination is essentially the only alternative. Saudi Arabia, for example, with no year-round rivers and only limited (and rapidly disappearing) groundwater, produces 70 percent of its fresh water from the sea, and pipes much of it long distances from the coasts on the Red Sea and the Persian Gulf to cities in the interior like Riyadh, the capital. Until recently the combination of desperation, wealth, and cheap energy has generally been regarded as representing a rare constellation of ingredients in which desalination might make sense.

The basic process isn't new; military vessels and cruise ships have relied on desalination for years. Worldwide, more than 13,000 desalination plants are in operation, producing 6.8 billion gallons a day. The largest, including one in Yuma, Arizona, tend to be those that purify brackish water, usually from underground, a process that is cheaper and easier than leaching salt from the far more saline seas. Most such plants can get away with systems that rely on heat, evaporation, and distillation. But seawater generally requires more, in technology and expense.

Remember high school science and osmosis, in which two bodies of water with different amounts of salt or other minerals will equalize in concentration? The most widely used process for seawater desalination uses reverse osmosis to accomplish the opposite, requiring 100,000 pounds per square inch of pressure as the seawater is pumped into plastic membranes through which salt and other molecules cannot pass. The reverse-osmosis membranes today cost half as much, last twice as long, and are twice as productive as membranes manufactured ten years ago, which is one reason that the price of the process has begun to drop. The other essential components are energy (to create the pressure) and a pipe infrastructure (to siphon water from the sea and return the discharge).

One lesson from Saudi Arabia has been that costs can be reduced when the desalination plant is built next to a coastal power plant, which provides cheap electricity and already relies on seawater for cooling. Nearly every seawater desalination plant now being planned or built, including those in Tampa (next to Tampa Electric Co.'s Big Bend plant) and San Diego County (next to the Encina Power Station, in Carlsbad, California), follows this model, including the use of power pump pipes and creating the arguable aesthetic benefit of putting one coastal eyesore next to another.

The widespread expectation is that the desalination market will increase quickly in coming years. Tampa, for one, is talking about building a second desalination plant; in California, as many as a dozen plants are expected to begin operations over the next ten years; nine water districts in south Texas have submitted proposals to meet increasing demands. In the United States today, the market for desalination plants and equipment is merely two billion dollars, but it may well grow to more than seventy billion dollars over the next two decades, according to the American Water Works Association, a major industry group. One of the biggest companies involved is Poseidon Resources, a privately held concern that was the lead developer on the Tampa Bay project, and which is also working on projects in San Diego and Huntington Beach, California, and Freeport, Texas.

What has changed, apart from the fact that desalinating seawater has become cheaper? One factor, as Adan Ortega, Jr., a vice president of the Metropolitan Water District of Southern California, put it, is that its alternatives as new sources of water have all become more expensive. The price of pulling water from existing reservoirs and streams is a tiny fraction of desalination.

But if it is possible at all, building new dams, pumping from new aquifers, or tapping existing rivers is becoming prohibitively expensive because of scarcity as well as regulatory and environmental hurdles. In one sign of public readiness to pay a price for desalination, California voters in November 2002 approved state funding for such efforts. That has allowed the Metropolitan Water District to back up its advocacy with money, by offering water districts like San Diego's subsidies of up to $250 per acre foot.

But even such a subsidy would go only a small way toward helping out with the price tag. In San Diego, current estimates for the facility planned for 2007 put the cost of desalting seawater at about $900 an acre foot, or $2.76 per 1,000 gallons. That is more than the cost at the older plant in Tampa, in part because the Pacific is saltier than Tampa Bay, and in part because Florida is flatter than southern California, reducing distribution costs. (Uphill pumping makes seawater desalination a solution primarily for the coasts.) The projected cost of desalinated seawater in San Diego is also nearly three times greater than the price of the transfer the county has negotiated with Imperial Valley farmers, and higher as well than some other options, including conservation and expanded groundwater production. Still, Bob Yamada, seawater desalination manager for the San Diego County Water Authority, argues that desalination makes sense, in part because it will "provide us with a new, local, high-quality, drought-proof supply that will help us to diversify our water-supply portfolio." No matter how little rain falls, no matter how much the levels of reservoirs, aquifers, and rivers drop, the ocean will be there.

Like most American communities, San Diego has been forced in recent years to confront its water future, and its projections look very different from the past and present. According to the Water Authority's current projections, demand in San Diego County will soar by about 33 percent by 2020, to 813,000 acre feet a year. The current blueprint calls for meeting it through a large shift away from imported water to local sources, and seawater (up from 0 percent to as much as 14 percent of supply) looms large among them. But it is important to note, too, that the plan also envisions a big leap in conservation (from one percent to 10 percent of supplies), recycling (from one percent to 6 percent), and the transfer of water from farmlands to the city (from 0 percent to 22 percent), and even increases in local surface water (from 3 percent to 6 percent) and aquifer (from 3 percent to 6 percent) supplies. The goal is greater self-sufficiency, to reduce dependence on others, particularly the overtapped Colorado River.

Alchemy or salvation? Maybe the better way to think about desalination is instead as just one part of the portfolio, one variable in the troublesome (and increasingly expensive) new balances that people around the world are seeking to strike when meeting water needs. "We live in an era where there is no free water, with increasing uncertainties caused by nature, politics, and regulation," said Adan Ortega, Jr. "The solution is diversity."

Barry Nelson, the water expert at the Natural Resources Defense Council, put it another way: "There is something primally appealing about turning salt water into fresh water. There is something almost biblical about that. And Americans love

whiz-bang technology. But my concern is that too much attention will leave people to forget about things like better shower-
heads and more water-efficient gardens. People are not laughing
at desalination any more. But it's not a silver bullet."

AFTERWORD

Bernadette McDonald

The world's water crisis is one of the most important challenges facing humanity at the beginning of the 21st century. The gravity of the situation is echoed time and time again in newspaper headlines, thoughtful editorials, television documentaries, G8 summits, coffee shop discussions, and environmental conferences. The crisis is enormous and complex, affecting over six billion people, with issues of scarcity and of quality, of governance and of ownership. There are no easy answers to the problems concerning this basic yet precious natural resource, and it seems at times that humanity has retreated into a kind of paralysis when trying to cope with the magnitude and complexity of the problem.

Secretary-General Kofi Annan was referring to many aspects of our environment, including water, when he said at the Johannesburg Summit in 2002: "It is said that to everything, there is a season. The world today needs to usher in a season of transformation, a season of stewardship. Let it be a season in which we make a long overdue investment in the survival and security of future generations." In addition to this call to action, the secretary-general had some words of warning: "And let us face an uncomfortable truth: the model of development we are accustomed to has been fruitful for the few, but flawed for the many. A path to prosperity that ravages the environment and leaves a majority of humankind behind in squalor will soon prove to be a dead-end road for everyone."

He went on to suggest methods expressed by many of the authors in this collection. He stressed the importance of education, working with technology, cooperation between government and the private sector, and leadership by the richest countries in the world, particularly, by the governments of those rich nations. He emphasized the inclusion of advocacy groups and watchdogs, as well as individual citizens. Most of all he stressed action—not tomorrow, but today.

Declarations of intent, concern, and action are not new. A steady parade of well-meaning statements has emanated from global gatherings of some of the most informed people on these topics. Not all of their intentions have been realized, but this does not minimize the importance of what has been said and the efforts that have been mobilized.

One of the more notable declarations came from the 1992 International Conference on Water and the Environment in Dublin, which created the four Dublin Principles. The first principle stated that fresh water is a finite and vulnerable resource, essential to sustain life, development, and the environment. The second principle urged that water development and management be based on a participatory approach, involving users, planners, and policymakers at all levels. The British Columbia Hydro methodology described by Hans Schreier is a good example of this more inclusive approach to water management. The third principle stressed that women should play a central part in the provision, management, and safeguarding of water. Sheila Patel's work with women in the villages of India proves that this approach works. The fourth principle recognized that water has an economic value in all its competing uses. The principles are as valid today as they were in 1992.

A decisive moment in the recent history of water management occurred at the United Nations Conference on the Environment and Development (UNCED) in 1992. This meeting produced Agenda 21, which included seven action areas in fresh water, providing a road map for the evolution of water management practices.

Eight years later, the Ministerial Declaration of The Hague on Water Security in the 21st Century took place. It stated, "Water is vital for the life and health of people and ecosystems and a basic requirement for the development of countries, but around the world women, men and children lack access to adequate and safe water to meet their most basic needs. Water resources, and the related ecosystems that provide and sustain them, are under threat from pollution, unsustainable use, land-use changes, climate change and many other forces. The link between these threats and poverty is clear, for it is the poor who are hit first and hardest. This leads to one simple conclusion: business as usual is not an option." Margaret Catley-Carlson and Hans Schreier have given vivid examples of where these links are strongest—in the driest countries and in many mountain regions of the world.

The Hague Declaration went on to commit to a goal of providing water security for the 21st century: "This means ensuring that freshwater, coastal and related ecosystems are protected and improved; that sustainable development and political stability are promoted; that every person has access to enough safe water at an affordable cost to lead a healthy and productive life and that the vulnerable are protected from the risks of water-related hazards."

The challenges of this kind of global declaration are enormous and, at least to this point, have proved to be unattainable. The goal of providing access to safe and sufficient water and sanitation to all has not been met. Neither has the challenge of providing sufficient water for food production. The integrity of ecosystems has clearly not been ensured through sustainable water resource management—another goal of the Declaration. The challenges of interbasin and transboundary cooperation are perhaps the most successful of all the declaration goals, as many of these tensions are being defused.

One of the more difficult goals was to determine the true value of water, its economic, social, environmental, and cultural value. This is also a work in progress. And like the secretary-general's statements, the declaration recommended that good water governance include all stakeholders in the decision-making process. In reality, a tug-of-war between private and public control of water has ensued.

Sound decisions about water are based on a thorough understanding of the hydrologic cycle and the part that human intervention plays in this cycle. The first important fact is that only 2.5 percent of all water is fresh water, and of that 2.5 percent, two-thirds of it is stored in glaciers and permanent snow. Water experts also tell us that most water resources are renewable—to a point. The cycle of precipitation, evapotranspiration, and runoff is one that should keep the water balance even. Healthy forests can assist this hydrologic equation, as Mike Dombeck explains in his essay. But human intervention has skewed the numbers somewhat. We use 8 percent of the total annual renewable fresh water and 26 percent of annual evapotranspiration, as well as 54 percent of accessible runoff. This amount of intervention is tipping the balance, resulting in what is commonly being referred to as the water crisis. Population growth and our growing need for water suggest that this crisis is growing as well. The many examples in China are a clear illustration.

In addition to overuse of fresh water, pollution further reduces supplies. Every day two million tons of industrial, agricultural, chemical, and human wastes are deposited into water supplies. The examples provided by experts throughout the essays in this collection are horrifyingly frequent.

Adding to the pressure is climate change. Precise impacts are still difficult to predict with certainty, but some recent studies suggest that climate change will, overall, account for approximately a 20 percent increase in global scarcity of fresh water by the middle of this century.

With all of these dire and yet informed predictions, now is the time for choice about how water needs of the future are going to be dealt with. Fundamental questions are being asked about whether the choice is to find more and more water, or to look at the existing supplies and begin to be smarter about how to use them.

One place to begin is with sanitation. Water-related diseases kill an estimated 10,000 to 20,000 children each day, mostly the poor in developing countries. Cholera, dengue fever, and arsenic-contaminated water are killing people; such deaths are preventable through better sanitation. The 1.1 billion people who lack access to an improved water supply and the 2.4 billion who need improved sanitation feed this vicious cycle of poverty and disease.

Perhaps nowhere in the world is this problem more menacing than in urban environments. Forty-eight percent of the world's population live in towns and cities, and this figure is expected to rise to 60 percent by 2030. In many of these urban areas, good waste management doesn't exist. The result is some of the world's most dangerous environments imaginable, places where disease thrives. This problem is then exported to downstream communities that have absolutely no influence over what is happening to their water supply upstream.

The tensions that result can flare between communities, watersheds, or countries. Since a complete watershed includes both the surface water and groundwater, there is much to share. It is unusual for a watershed boundary to coincide with an administrative boundary. But despite the potential for serious conflict, the current situation is surprisingly cooperative. In the past 50 years, 1,200 cooperative interactions around water have taken place, as opposed to 500 conflicts over water.

United Nations studies have found that, although water wars have been predicted, particularly in the Middle East, most conflicts have been settled through diplomacy. Perhaps, at this level, water is regarded as too fundamental to life to fight over. Within countries, however, negotiations over who has the greatest access to watershed resources remain tough and protracted. In many cases, the greatest battles are fought over water for food. Or in the case of the Colorado River, the lengthiest negotiations are conducted over water for food.

Tension over water for food should not come as a surprise, since the world's food supply comes primarily from agriculture. Although most agriculture is rainfed, irrigation is very important and growing ever more so. At the moment, 70 percent of all water use is for irrigation. Much irrigation water comes from shallow groundwater, and this is creating a serious and growing problem. Overpumping of aquifers is resulting in dramatic aquifer problems, as in China and Texas, and pollution of aquifers from agricultural chemicals is aggravating the situation.

Although agriculture is by far the greatest user of fresh water at the moment, industry is a growing consumer. By 2025, industry will increase its water usage to 24 percent of all water consumed. This water is being used for a variety of purposes, and unfortunately all too often after it has been used in industry, it is returned to water systems inadequately treated. This threatens both surface water and groundwater. Even though industry is now beginning to use wastewater, its final discharge back into the watershed still must be adequately treated. Huge increases of industrial use of water are expected in developing countries where industrial development is booming. The future challenge of controlling the amount of inadequately treated water streaming back into the watersheds will be critical.

Another growing consumer of water is the energy sector, particularly the generation of hydroelectricity. Hydroelectric power currently represents only 19 percent of total electricity production. There is still opportunity for expansion in this sector, much of which also rests in developing countries, since that is where most of the economically feasible hydropower sites exist. It also appears that the future may be primarily with small-scale hydropower projects. These smaller stand-alone plants generate less that 10 megawatts and are plagued with fewer of the problems associated with large plants. By 2010, these kinds of small developments are expected to grow by 60 percent.

As human needs for water continue to increase, the full value of water needs to be understood. It's clear that water has economic value, but its overall value includes environmental, cultural, and religious considerations as well. What is even more complex is that these are often interrelated.

A reoccurring mantra from every major water study and water congress held in recent years is the urgent need for capital investment. Although public funding is an ongoing need, more private investments in water infrastructure are being made. In fact, the second World Water Forum in The Hague in 2000 recognized the need for more involvement by the private sector, particularly since the World Bank has estimated that more than 60 billion dollars of investment for water infrastructure is needed each year for the next decade. There are a number of international private water companies, but two French multinational corporations dominate the sector: Vivendi SA and Suez Lyonnaise des Eaux. These own or have interests in water projects in more than 120 countries. But heated debate has arisen on what exactly the acceptable rates of return are, in the form of profits, to the private sector given a resource as fundamental as water. This includes serious concerns about how the water needs of the poor are protected. Maude Barlow's studies on water privatization reveal some sobering examples of highly controversial failures in this area. Push-back, protests, and sometimes violence have been the result of privatization schemes that have gone wrong in Bolivia, South Africa, and the Philippines.

A more integrated approach is gathering momentum where government agencies, private companies, and individuals are working together to find the required capital investments as well as to fully understand the water-related needs of people. More complete long-term solutions are found when all of the voices of those who use water are heard. This is a philosophy of devolution of authority from a centralized government infrastructure to the communities who use the water.

Most experts agree that, despite the growing importance of the private sector, governments must continue to have the fundamental responsibility for basic services such as water, sewerage, and energy. Transferring this responsibility to the private sector is not seen as viable, particularly with the poor. Some privatization schemes without proper government control have charged the poor far more for questionable water than other middle-class customers pay for clean water.

This demonstrates the fundamental work that still needs to be done to fully understand the value of water; its cultural, religious, and ecological value cannot be determined by market forces. Unfortunately, it's in places where governments are weakest and where people are poorest that privatization efforts are growing, not always to the benefit of all.

The importance of good governance on water issues cannot be overstated. Regulations, laws, monitoring, access, upstream/downstream impacts, full-value costing, delivery systems, conflicting interests—all are part of the mix that policymakers must consider in a responsible, ethical, and equitable process. At least some of the impetus for proper controls will come from the public. Public interest in water issues has probably never been keener. Advancing that interest to knowledge of the local issues involved will be vital in informing decisions about water management for the future. That knowledge has to embrace many sectors: health, agriculture, industry, energy, ecosystem managers, scientists, educators, private water companies, and government officials. It has to be disseminated to all countries, including those who can't afford to seek it out, and it needs to be taught at the youngest possible levels.

Because the water crisis is at the heart of our survival, inspired leadership is required to solve it. Some words from Secretary-General Kofi Annan at his Johannesburg Summit presentation give a sense of the scope of leadership required: "If there is one word that should be on everyone's lips at this summit, one concept that embodies everything we hope to achieve here in Johannesburg, it is responsibility. Responsibility for each other—but especially the poor, the vulnerable, and the oppressed—as fellow members of a single human family. Responsibility for our planet, whose bounty is the very basis for human well-being and progress. And most of all, responsibility for the future—for our children, and their children."

There are people taking responsibility for the future: Sheila Patel's work with the women in India, British Columbia Hydro's participatory approach, the mountain sculptors in Nepal, farmers who use drip irrigation, scientists like David Schindler. The authors in this collection have given us examples of individuals and organizations building on existing knowledge and acting accordingly. The challenge now is to learn from those examples that work and repeat them—as often as is necessary. Like any massive and complex project, all the pieces that make up the whole must be grasped and applied in a logical manner so that the ecological balance in the world's water crisis is tipped—this time in the right direction. It's our responsibility to change our attitudes about water, to learn from failures, and to build on successes for future generations and for the planet.

NOTES

Maude Barlow

[1] Adapted from Barlowe, Maude, and Clark, Tony, "Who Owns Water?" *The Nation*, September 2-9, 2002: pp. 11-14.

[2] ibid.

[3] Percentages and other data derived from Public Citizen: www.citizen.org/cmep/ water/cmep_water/reports/organization/articles.cfm?ID=9207.

Lester R. Brown

Adapted from Lester R. Brown, *Plan B: Rescuing a Planet under Stress and a Civilization in Trouble* (W.W. Norton & Co., New York: 2003).

Hans Schreier

[1] Krajick, 2002

[2] Thompson et al., 2002

[3] Sharma et. al., 2000

[4] von Westarp, 2001

[5] Mastny, 2001

[6] Pleumaron, 1997; UNESCO, 2000

[7] Walder, 2000; Baroni et al., 1998

[8] Price et al., 1997

[9] World Commission on Dams, 2002

[10] Stockner et al., 2000

Mike Dombeck

This chapter draws on M. Dombeck (2002), "Protecting the Stuff of Life," *Wisconsin Academy Review* 48(1):14-18; and M. Dombeck, C. Wood, and J. Williams (2003), *From Conquest to Conservation: Our Public Lands Legacy*, Island Press, Washington, D.C.

[1] Percentages from "A clear-cut drought solution?" by Theo Stein, *Denver Post*, November 10, 2002.

Peter H. Gleick

[1] http://www.cityofseattle.net/util/services/Drinkingwater/docs/Usage2001.PDF

[2] The term "soft path" was first used by Amory Lovins in the late 1970s to describe an energy transition that shifted the focus of energy policymakers from energy supply to energy demand. Many of the concepts and ideas around a soft path for water are similar, though water has some unique characteristics.

[3] A more comprehensive discussion of the "soft path" for water can be found in P.H. Gleick (2002), "Soft water paths," *Nature* 418 (July 25): 373; G. Wolff and P.H. Gleick (2002), "The soft path for water"; and P.H. Gleick (editor), *The World's Water 2002-2003*, Island Press, Washington, D.C.

[4] These data are all in 1990 Hong Kong dollars. The data are available in P.H. Gleick (2002), *The World's Water 2002-2003*, Island Press, Washington, D.C., and come from D.Y. Chen at the Chinese University of Hong Kong.

[5] These data are corrected for inflation (1992 U.S. dollars).

[6] Data on steel manufacturing in the 1930s and 1940s can be found in National

Association of Manufacturers (1950), *Water in industry*, Economics Policy Division Series, No. 36, Appendix C. Data from the Pohang and Gwangyang Works in Korea can be found at http://www.posco.co.kr/en/news/News_view.

[7] http://www.cabq.gov/progress/EP03PERC.html

[8] http://www.nyc.gov/html/dep/html/droughthist.html

[9] A.L. Vickers (2001), *Handbook of Water Use and Conservation*, WaterPlow Press, Amherst, Massachusetts.

[10] IPTRID (2001), *Case Studies on Water Conservation in the Mediterranean Region*, International Programme for Technology and Research in Irrigation and Drainage, FAO, Rome, Italy.

[11] S. Postel (1999), *Pillar of Sand. Can the Irrigation Miracle Last?* W.W. Norton and Co., New York.

[12] Op. cit. IPTRID, 2001.

[13] Total irrigated area is estimated to be around 275 million hectares. Global area under micro-irrigation has been estimated at around 2.8 million hectares. (D. Bucks, U.S. Department of Agriculture, cited by S. Postel, P. Polak, F. Gonzales, and J. Keller (2001), "Drip irrigation for small farmers," *Water International;* Vol. 26 (I): 3-13.

[14] P.H. Gleick (1999), "Crop shifting in California: Increasing farmer revenue, decreasing farm water use." In L. Owens-Viani, A.K. Wong, and P.H. Gleick (editors), *Sustainable Use of Water: California Success Stories*, Pacific Institute for Studies in Development, Environment, and Security, Oakland, California, pp.149-163.

[15] The World Health Organization estimates that 2.4 billion people lacked "adequate" sanitation in 2000. See World Health Organization (2000), *Global Water Supply and Sanitation Assessment 2000 Report*, WHO/UNICEF Joint Monitoring Programme for Water Supply and Sanitation, Geneva, Switzerland (available at http://www.who.int/water_sanitation_health/Globassessment/GlobalToc.htm). Population in 1940 was estimated by the United Nations at 2.3 billion. United Nations (1966), *World Population Prospects as Assessed in 1963*, United Nations Publication, New York.

ABOUT THE AUTHORS

Best-selling author MAUDE BARLOW is national chairperson of The Council of Canadians, Canada's largest public-advocacy organization. A director with the International Forum on Globalization, a San Francisco–based institution opposed to economic globalization, she is co-founder of the Blue Planet Project, an international civil-society movement fighting the commodification of water.

LESTER R. BROWN is president of Earth Policy Institute and founder and former president of the Worldwatch Institute. During a career that began with tomato farming, Brown has been awarded over 20 honorary degrees and has written or co-written some 30 books, including *Eco-Economy: Building an Economy for the Earth*. He is also a MacArthur fellow and the recipient of the 1987 United Nations Environment Prize, the 1989 World Wide Fund for Nature Gold Medal, and the 1994 Blue Planet Prize for his "exceptional contributions to solving global environmental problems."

MARGARET CATLEY-CARLSON is chair of the Global Water Partnership, a global network of water-management professionals. Her 35-year career in economic development has included terms as president of the Canadian International Development Agency, deputy director of UNICEF, and chair of the Geneva-based Water Supply Sanitation Collaborative Council.

MARQ DE VILLIERS is the recipient of a 1999 Governor General's Literary Award for his book *Water*. Currently editorial director of *Where Magazine International*, he was formerly the publisher of *Toronto Life Magazine*.

MIKE DOMBECK was chief of the Forest Service and director of the Bureau of Land Management and is now professor of global environmental management at the University of Wisconsin, Stevens Point, and UW System Fellow of Global Conservation.

PETER H. GLEICK is co-founder and president of the Pacific Institute for Studies in Development, Environment, and Security in Oakland, California, one of the world's leading nonpartisan policy research groups addressing global environment and development problems, especially in the area of freshwater research. Dr. Gleick's work on sustainable management and use of water led to his being named by the BBC as a "visionary on the environment" in its *Essential Guide to the 21st Century*. Dr. Gleick is an academician of the International Water Academy, Oslo, Norway, and a member of the Water Science and Technology Board of the U.S. National Academy of Sciences.

ROBERT GLENNON is a professor of law and public policy at the University of Arizona in Tucson. He specializes in constitutional law, American legal history, and water law. He is the author of *Water Follies: Groundwater Pumping and the Fate of America's Fresh Water.*

As counselor to the secretary of the interior from 1997 to 1999, and then deputy secretary of the interior from 1999 to 2001, DAVID J. HAYES played a key role in negotiations over the Colorado River. He is a former chairman of the board of the Environmental Law Institute and a current board member of American Rivers, the National Heritage Institute, and Stanford Law School Board of Visitors.

DAVID SCHINDLER is a professor of ecology at the University of Alberta whose work has been widely used in formulating ecologically sound management policy in North America and Europe. His current research includes the effects of climate change and ultraviolet radiation on lakes.

A professor at the Institute for Resources and Environment at the University of British Columbia, HANS SCHREIER has dedicated much of his research time to water and resource issues in the Himalaya and Andes. He has developed CD-ROMs on mountain processes as well as Internet-based courses on watershed management.

Internationally respected geneticist DAVID SUZUKI, chair of the David Suzuki Foundation, is an award-winning scientist and environmentalist who has received high acclaim for 30 years of work in broadcasting, explaining the complexities of science.

AARON WOLF is an associate professor of geography in the Department of Geosciences at Oregon State University. He has acted as consultant to the U.S. Department of State, the U.S. Agency for International Development, and the World Bank on various aspects of transboundary water resources and dispute resolution. He is the author of *Hydropolitics Along the Jordan River: The Impact of Scarce Water Resources on the Arab-Israeli Conflict* and a co-director of the Universities Partnership on Transboundary Waters.

BANFF MOUNTAIN SUMMIT

MOUNTAINS AS WATER TOWERS

NOVEMBER 23-26, 2003

An event to celebrate the importance of fresh water during the United Nations International Year of Freshwater, the summit explores issues surrounding the great storage houses of fresh water in mountain regions of the world. The summit looks at a 20-year horizon and includes many of the renowned authors in this book: People whose expertise and passion for clean water for the 21st century has translated into creative endeavors, scientific research, and critical thinking.

The summit is presented by The Walter & Duncan Gordon Foundation, and sponsored by Parks Canada, Petro-Canada, Environment Canada, and Health Canada; National Geographic; The Calgary Foundation; TD Friends of the Environment Foundation; Bow River Basin Council; and Western Economic Diversification Canada. The summit is offered in cooperation with Partners for the Saskatchewan River Basin, the International Development Research Centre, Alberta Ecotrust, and the Mountain Forum (North American node).

Presented by

Sponsored by

 Government   Gouvernement
of Canada   du Canada

PETRO-CANADA

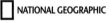 NATIONAL GEOGRAPHIC

THE CALGARY
FOUNDATION

 Friends of the
Environment
Foundation

Bow River
BASIN

Council

In cooperation with

 IDRC ✳ CRDI
International Development   Centre de recherches pour le
Research Centre   développement international

 Mountain Forum

alberta
ecotrust

Partners FOR the

Saskatchewan
River Basin

ACKNOWLEDGMENTS

We are grateful to many who believed in and supported this literary collection recognizing the International Year of Freshwater. Thank you to the remarkable authors and scientists who have informed and challenged us through their essays. Kevin Mulroy and Johnna Rizzo of NG Books embraced this project and nurtured it through to completion. The financial support of our sponsors helped make this book possible. The Banff Centre Mountain Culture team provided Bernadette with the quiet time and support to close office doors and concentrate on the words; the *New York Times* offered understanding and encouragement. And once again, project coordinator Paula Rondina was unceasing in her efforts to get it done on time. Thank you all.

Bernadette McDonald and Doug Jehl